SAINT BONIFACE

SAINT BONIFACE

Three Biographical Studies for the Twelfth Centenary Festival

BY

GEORGE WILLIAM GREENAWAY, M.A.

LECTURER IN MEDIEVAL HISTORY
UNIVERSITY COLLEGE OF THE SOUTH-WEST OF ENGLAND

"Si mihi tantummodo solida inesset voluntas, a Domino cetera prestari"—Othlo, Prologue to *Life of St Boniface*.

LONDON
ADAM AND CHARLES BLACK

FIRST PUBLISHED 1955

A. AND C. BLACK LTD
4, 5 AND 6 SOHO SQUARE LONDON W.1

TO THE PEOPLE
OF ST JAMES'
EXETER

Made in Great Britain
Printed by W. & J. Mackay & Co. Ltd., Chatham

FOREWORD

BY THE LORD BISHOP OF EXETER
THE RT. REVD. R. C. MORTIMER, D.D.

No short and scholarly life of St Boniface exists in English. When I began to prepare for the celebration of the Twelfth Centenary of the Martyrdom of St Boniface I saw at once the need for a book of this kind, that ordinary lay members of the Church of England might be reasonably informed of what it is intended to celebrate. The people of England know far too little about one who has recently been described by Christopher Dawson in *The Making of Europe* in these terms: "A man who had a deeper influence on the history of Europe than any Englishman who has ever lived." Sir Arthur Bryant in *The Story of England* says of St Boniface: "No Englishman's work has had a greater influence on the world."

I was, accordingly, very grateful to Mr Greenaway for undertaking, at my request, the writing of this short life of St Boniface. It is a fitting and important part of our celebrations and a just tribute by his native Church of England to his memory.

CONTENTS

PREFACE

This book has been written for the Exeter Diocesan Festival of 1955 in commemoration of the Twelfth Centenary of Saint Boniface and in the hope of arousing fresh interest in the life and work of a great Englishman and a great saint. No biography of St Boniface has appeared in English since the publication of Bishop G. F. Browne's *Boniface of Crediton and His Companions* in 1910. In the past forty years some important new material has come to hand, and individual scholars have made a closer study of the saint's correspondence and the contemporary *Lives* of him and his fellow workers in the German mission field. This has thrown fresh light on the man and his personality, and on his multifarious activities as a Christian missionary and an ecclesiastical statesman. In consequence it is now possible to measure more accurately both the significance of Boniface's achievement for his own time and his legacy to Western Christendom in the Middle Ages. The present book, necessarily limited in size, is intended primarily for the general reader without special knowledge of the subject. It is based, however, on a study of the original sources and incorporates many of the new ideas and interpretations emanating from recent historical writing on the period. It consists of three studies, each dealing with one of the chief phases or aspects of the saint's life and work. As far as possible, particularly in the first two studies, a proper biographical sequence has been maintained. The references in the text to the *Letters* are to the numeration adopted by M. Tangl in his edition of the original Latin published in 1916 and followed by E. Emerton and C. H. Talbot in their versions in English.

I desire to express my thanks to Dr Frank Barlow, Professor of History in the University College of the South-West, for his initial suggestion as to the form the book should take, and to record my appreciation of the interest shown by him and my other colleagues on the staff of the History Department in the progress of the work. My wife has somehow found time to read these pages and has helped me by doing so more than she knows; to her also I offer thanks.

GEORGE W. GREENAWAY

University College, Exeter

Epiphany, 1955

I. BONIFACE AS A CHRISTIAN MISSION-ARY: THE "APOSTLE OF GERMANY"

In the published correspondence of St Boniface there is to be found a remarkable letter (*Ep.* 111 in Tangl's edition) written by Cuthbert, archbishop of Canterbury, to the Englishman Lull (or Lullus), the disciple, fellow-worker and friend of Boniface, and his chosen successor in the see of Mainz. It is more than an official letter of condolence on the death of Boniface; it is a veritable panegyric of the martyred saint. It illustrates not only the high esteem and personal affection in which he was held by the bishops and churchmen of his native land, but also their pride in this great Christian leader and evangelist of the Anglo-Saxon race. "We render thanks to God"—so wrote the archbishop —"that the English people, foreigners though they be, were judged worthy to send forth this gifted student of heavenly learning, this noble soldier of Christ, together with so many disciples well taught and trained, to engage in distant warfare for the salvation of many souls and the praise of Almighty God." Like a true champion and standard-bearer, the letter continues, this great Apostle has carried the message of the gospel into the most remote and inaccessible places, where no preacher before him had ever penetrated, and by the inspiration of his words and the example of his holy life he has succeeded in bringing whole nations, and among them the most barbarous, out of the darkness of ignorance and superstition into the glorious light of the gospel of Jesus Christ. Archbishop Cuthbert then informs Lull that a recent synod of the English Church has decreed that the day of the saint's martyrdom (5th June) shall be

solemnly commemorated annually, and that he shall henceforth be ranked, together with Gregory the Great and
Augustine, as one of the three patrons of the English Church.

Here, in this official proclamation, we have the yard-
stick by which his Anglo-Saxon contemporaries measured
the achievement of Boniface. Today, as we look back over
the long vistas of European civilisation, an even higher
place in history may confidently be assigned to him. He may
be acclaimed, not only as the "Apostle of Germany"—a
title already accorded him in his own day—but also, in
Christopher Dawson's words, as "a man who had a deeper
influence on the history of Europe than any Englishman
who has ever lived". For not only did Boniface plant
Christianity firmly in the soil of Germany, but he was
responsible, more than any other man, for planting with it
the Romano-Christian civilisation of the early Middle Ages
in lands where the Roman legions had never trod. This in
itself is sufficient to warrant his inclusion among the select
company of "makers of the Middle Ages".

The seventh century, into which Boniface was born, was
a troubled and disordered period for Western Europe as a
whole no less than for England, his native land. It was very
much the "Dark Ages", though here and there the darkness
was lifting a little and a grey morning twilight ushering in
the none too roseate sunrise of the medieval world. It was
unmistakably an age of transition between the ancient
Roman world that was dying or dead and the new Romano-
Barbarian world that seemed, in Matthew Arnold's phrase,
"powerless to be born". Two hundred years ago the Roman
Empire in the West, with its vaunted *Pax Romana* and its
unified system of law and administration, had collapsed
under pressure from the Teutonic invaders beyond the
Rhine and the Danube, and out of the welter and anarchy
consequent upon its disruption had emerged, slowly and
painfully, a number of independent tribal and Teutonic
kingdoms in Italy, North Africa, Spain and Gaul. The city

of Rome, though steadily growing in prestige as the great Christian metropolis of the West, was never again the political capital of a Roman Empire, and by the beginning of the seventh century the Lombards, the last of the Teutonic invaders from beyond the Alps, were pouring into northern Italy and threatening to turn Rome into an Arian and barbarian capital to the peril alike of the religious orthodoxy and the political independence of the Papacy. Farther west the eighth century was to see the fanatical warriors of Islam from North Africa overrun almost the whole of the Iberian peninsula and cross the Pyrenees into Aquitaine, thereby threatening the total destruction of Catholic Christendom by an attack on its western flank. From this dire peril Christian Europe was to be saved by Charles Martel's victory on the field of Poitiers in 732, and this event was but one of several indications that the future destinies of Western Europe were to be entrusted to the Franks.

For alone among the young barbarian kingdoms established in the fifth century on the ruins of the Roman Empire that of Clovis had maintained its independence, prospered and expanded, despite the frequent partitions of its territory between his sons and grandsons, and the internecine feuds and moral degeneracy of the later Merovingian kings. The most important factors in this survival are undoubtedly the unity engendered by a common Catholic Faith shared by Franks and Gallo-Romans and the friendly relations with the pope at Rome which this entailed. The extension of the boundaries of Catholic Christendom thus came to be dependent upon, and inseparably linked with, the territorial expansion of the Frankish state. So it came about that the eighth century, which was to see so serious a contraction of the western frontier of Christendom through the loss of Spain to the followers of the Prophet, was also to witness the extension of the Catholic Faith eastwards beyond the Rhine among the heathen tribes of Germany beneath the protective cover of the Frankish armies.

The political geography of Anglo-Saxon England during the seventh century was scarcely less confused and complex than that of the European continent, though the scale of events and changes was naturally a good deal smaller. It was the England of the Heptarchy, marked by the rise and fall of one overlordship after another, in which no one kingdom or people succeeded in achieving a complete or permanent hegemony over its rivals. In rapid and bewildering succession, and consequent always upon the fortunes of war, the political leadership of the Anglo-Saxon peoples changed hands four times in the hundred years between 616 and 716, and the two larger states, Northumbria and Mercia, had each twice achieved a substantial, if limited, overlordship over the smaller tribal kingdoms of Kent, Sussex, Essex and East Anglia. The remaining kingdom of the Heptarchy, that of the West Saxons, played but a minor part in these confused struggles. Yet it is with the latter that we are here concerned, since Boniface was indisputably a son of Wessex. Unfortunately, the various stages in the growth and expansion of the Wessex kingdom are subject to considerable doubt and confusion. Well before the close of the sixth century the West Saxons had begun to push westwards and southwards from their original settlements on the middle and upper Thames, but exactly how far the advance had penetrated by the middle of the seventh century is an almost insoluble problem. Sir Frank Stenton is of opinion that already, before the victorious campaigns waged by King Ine against the Celts of the Dumnonian peninsula between 690 and 720, the western frontier of Wessex had been extended at least as far as the Devon-Somerset border, and perhaps as far as the Exe estuary. If this was so, Exeter may well have been the site of a Saxon settlement at an early date. The question is of some importance for its bearing on Boniface's early life and training, but there is unfortunately no strong or convincing evidence on the point. It is certain, however, that the main line of West Saxon expansion during the sixth and seventh centuries was in a south-westerly direction, away from the tribal settlements of the Thames valley towards the New Forest area and the Channel coast. Moreover, it is significant that by the middle of the seventh century the ancient city of Winchester had become both the political and ecclesiastical capital of Wessex, and it was with Winchester, and its bishop, Daniel, that the earliest activities of Boniface were closely linked.

At the close of the seventh century, then, Anglo-Saxon England seemed on the face of things to be no nearer the goal of political unification than at the beginning. The struggles for supremacy between the rival kingdoms were not yet at an end, and few could have anticipated the ultimate triumph of Wessex under Alfred and his successors. Yet each succeeding overlordship strengthened in the long run the forces making for cohesion and stability, and already these forces had received a potent stimulus from the religious unity proclaimed in the Synod of Whitby in 663 and made substantially effective in the years immediately following, thanks to the organising ability of Theodore of Tarsus, appointed archbishop of Canterbury in 669. These two events, the decision at Whitby to acknowledge the Roman obedience and the primacy of St Peter in preference to those of Celtic Iona and St Columba, and the coming of Theodore, which followed hard upon it, were of cardinal importance for the development of the Anglo-Saxon Church and scarcely less so for the political unification of the whole country. One by one the other kings of the Heptarchy followed the lead of Oswiu of Northumbria with the result that the ambition of Gregory the Great for a united Anglo-Saxon Church was at long last fulfilled. Under Archbishop Theodore the English Church formed an integral part of the Church Catholic, and the measures which he took to regularise the anomalous position of the existing bishops,

whether of Roman or Celtic appointment, to fill the many
vacant sees and to settle conflicting claims to others, to
divide the unwieldy tribal dioceses, to provide for annual
meetings of convocation in the two provinces of Canterbury
and York, to summon ecclesiastical councils for the purpose
of reforming abuses and legislating on faith, morals and
church order; all these multifarious activities were designed
to establish the English Church on a permanent and well-
ordered foundation. Theodore left as his memorial a Church
compact and harmonious, with its administration working
smoothly, with a diocesan episcopate firmly established on
a territorial basis and increasingly recruited from men of
Anglo-Saxon race, with both monks and secular priests reformed and disciplined, with clergy and lay folk alike
intensely active in building and endowing churches, schools
and monasteries, and in the first flush of religious enthusiasm
already "launching out into the deep" of continental
heathenism "to catch men" for Christ. Conscious of its new-
born integrity, the Anglo-Saxon Church was fast becoming
a potent and almost irresistible force in politics. The unity
of the Church became the pattern for the unity of the state.
The men of Wessex, Mercia and Northumbria, and of the
lesser kingdoms of the Heptarchy were becoming increasingly aware of their common heritage in everything per-
taining to religion and the things of God, even though in
their temporal occupations and interests they were still constrained by the lesser loyalties of tribe and folk and king.

This awareness of a common spiritual heritage enjoyed
by all of Anglo-Saxon race finds supreme expression in the
life and letters of St Boniface. He undoubtedly regarded his
apostolate as in some sense a common enterprise of the
whole English nation, and it was the traditional Anglo-
Saxon religious culture of the age of Bede which he strove
to inculcate into the schools and monasteries of the infant
German churches. The same is true of his work as an ecclesiastical organiser: the pattern to which he worked was

always that of the English Church as Theodore of Tarsus had shaped it.

But this is not all. Boniface was more than a mere protagonist of Anglo-Saxon religious culture on the European continent. He was also the spiritual son of the Celtic monk-missionaries who had brought the gospel and Christian learning from Ireland to Scotland with St Columba, from Scotland to Northumbria with St Aidan, and had blazed the trail in Gaul and Central Europe with St Columbanus and St Gall. Indeed he was more indebted to the Celtic saints than he ever recognised. His apostolate was a fitting symbol of that fusion between the Roman genius for order, discipline and obedience and the Celtic genius for personal sanctity, ascetic piety and fervid evangelism which took place in Anglo-Saxon Christianity in the generation following the Synod of Whitby. For, although the Celtic churchmen had been defeated by Wilfrid of Ripon and the Roman party over the momentous issues there debated, the inspiration of the Celtic genius continued to work powerfully in the life of the English Church. In process of time English Christianity incorporated all that was best and noblest in the ancient Celtic customs and traditions. Paramount among these were the conception of the religious life as an enlistment in the ranks of "Christ's militia" and a propensity to become wandering preachers in distant lands in literal obedience to the gospel precept. Thus, in the field of continental evangelism the Anglo-Saxon churchmen of the seventh century became heirs to the inheritance of Patrick, Columba and Aidan. Among those who may justly claim this high spiritual lineage are the "three W's", Wilfrid of Ripon (somewhat ironically), Willibrord of Northumbria and Winfrith of Crediton, better known as St Boniface. They take their places in chronological sequence and ascending order of magnitude.

The circumstances of Winfrith's birth, like those of many another saint and hero of the "Dark Ages", are wrapped

B

in obscurity. Neither the place nor the date can be determined with absolute certainty. A strong local tradition names Crediton as his birthplace, but the evidence for this is no older than the liturgical calendar of Bishop Grandisson of Exeter (1327–69), and the authority for the bishop's statement is unknown. Nevertheless, despite the absence of confirmatory evidence, this tradition may still be accepted, since it is almost certain that Winfrith was born somewhere near Exeter. According to the contemporary *Life* written by the Anglo-Saxon priest, Willibald, who himself worked in the German mission field and had access to good materials, the lad was committed by his parents at a tender age to a monastery at "Adescancastre" as an oblate, and there he received his early education. The identification of this place with Exeter appears sufficiently warranted. The actual date of Winfrith's birth is equally doubtful. Levison conjectures that it took place round about the year 675, but it may have been as early as 672 or as late as 680. He was certainly a very old man at the time of his martydom, and any date within the range given would be compatible with that fact. We know neither the names nor the condition of his parents, but it is likely that they were both of Anglo-Saxon race and of noble birth. Boniface's description of himself in one of his early letters as "the offspring of an ignoble stem" should not be taken literally as implying servile birth, for the phrase is an affectation of humility commonly employed by churchmen in that age. His father was a man of substance, and probably of thegnly rank. He may well have been connected with the Anglo-Saxon trading community already established in Exeter at this time. In Willibald's opening pages the father figures prominently in the story of Winfrith's boyhood. Nourished on the lives and legends of the saints and stimulated by the conversation of visiting priests and clerks who occasionally enjoyed his father's hospitality, the young child early "fell in love with religion". The desire to serve God in a monastery and to apply his talents to "Divine learning" grew in him with the years. In vain his father strove to dissuade him from this course and to entice him with the prospect of inheriting the family estates if he would consent to remain "in the world". The lad grew more and more importunate and recalcitrant, until the father, recognising the futility of further opposition, at last gave way and granted his son's request. So, with the consent of the whole family, the lad was sent off to the monastery at Exeter to receive schooling there from Abbot Wulfhard and his monks.

We know next to nothing about this monastery and little of Winfrith's life there. The house must have been small and of recent Saxon foundation containing a few clerks living under the Benedictine rule. The young Winfrith would be but one of several oblate children receiving education in the abbey school. He was an apt pupil, "endowed with a spark of divine genius", says Willibald, and soon became proficient in such elementary learning as his teachers could provide for him. But he fast outgrew this "primary school" and longed for the opportunity of continuing and expanding his studies in some more favourable environment. The standard of education in this frontier outpost of Wessex Christianity could not have been conspicuously high; the monastery was small and its library resources strictly limited. So, in early manhood and with the full consent of his abbot, he removed to the Benedictine house at Nursling near Southampton in search of higher learning and more competent teachers. Here, under the friendly and scholarly guidance of Abbot Winbert, whom he ever afterwards held in respect and affection, he found greater facilities both as student and as teacher. Devoting himself to the study of letters, both sacred (the Vulgate and the Latin Fathers) and secular (the Latin classics), he rapidly became a proficient Latin scholar and, from evidence in his correspondence, he also acquired some knowledge of Greek. His fame as a teacher soon spread far beyond the confines of his own

monastery, especially after he had become head of the abbey
school. In exposition and commentary of the Bible he was
unsurpassed in his immediate circle, and many (monks and
nuns) were drawn from neighbouring religious houses to
seek instruction from him both in sacred learning and in the
discipline of the "religious" life. His work as a teacher
necessarily involved attempts at original composition. Some
of his early efforts in this field have come down to us. They
include Latin elegiac verses, Latin riddles and acrostics,
which he did much to popularise, a Latin grammar and a
treatise on metrics intended for use in the classroom. By
this time he had fallen under the spell of the presiding
genius of West Saxon learning, Aldhelm, abbot of Malmesbury and later bishop of Sherborne, and these literary exercises of his youth are but servile imitations of the ornate and
pompous style of the master. But he soon emancipated himself from Aldhelm and ultimately made in his *Letters* his own
specific contribution to the progress of Anglo-Saxon learning, as will be shown in the third essay. The chief point to
note here is that Willibald's account of Winfrith's education at Nursling affords, in S. J. Crawford's words, "a
valuable glimpse of the extensive range of studies pursued
at a comparatively small Anglo-Saxon monastery in the
early eighth century".

In learning and literature, then, Winfrith at Nursling
progressed according to the best traditions of the age of
Aldhelm and Bede. Equally marked, according to Willibald,
was his progress in the spiritual life. "He was an example of
Christian life and a perfect model of apostolic learning. He
trod in the footsteps of the saints, and climbed the steep
path that leads to knowledge of heavenly things." In the
cloister he practised the ascetic virtues of self-discipline and
abstinence which were the secret of his life as a man of
prayer, and enabled him to become a true spiritual mentor
to his brother-monks and the novices placed under his care.
It is important to realise that he was now, and ever after-

wards remained, first and foremost a monk, a gifted exponent of the "religious" life, the pattern and exemplar of all that was best in the monastic life of the age. In all his future labours as an evangelist he remained unswervingly true to his calling as a monk. Moreover, he was a *Benedictine* monk, imbued with that sense of discipline, obedience and ordered community life within the fold of the Catholic Church which was the distinguishing feature of the Benedictine Order. This was not the least of the lessons taught him by his experience of life in the cloister at Exeter and Nursling. At the canonical age of thirty he was ordained priest and soon became no less renowned as a preacher than as a teacher. As an ordained priest, dwelling in a community whose members were probably mostly laymen, he soon made wider contacts and enlarged his practical experience of West Saxon church life. Evidently he was regarded as "a coming man", for at a synod of Wessex clergy held under King Ine some time between 710 and 712 he was chosen, on the joint nomination of his own abbot, Winbert, and the abbots of Tisbury and Glastonbury, to carry the synodal decrees to Canterbury for approval and confirmation by Archbishop Bertwald. He acquitted himself so well in this mission that he was regularly invited to attend later synods and employed as an envoy on similar occasions. He was by now personally known to his diocesan, Bishop Daniel of Winchester, and the foundations of the latter's respect and admiration were laid in these early years. Everything pointed to a useful and prosperous, perhaps even a distinguished, career as a leader in the ecclesiastical politics of Wessex. But there was that in Winfrith which could never be satisfied with achieving personal distinction even in a sacred profession. He had begun to nurse ambitions of a higher, more spiritual order. He felt stirring within him "immortal longings" which could never be realised in his provincial homeland. Son of Wessex though he was, he had caught some of the "Celtic fire" from the emigrant

Irish saints and scholars who had sailed overseas to spread
the gospel far and wide in Germany and central Europe. If
some part of this enthusiasm be accounted visionary or
idealistic, it was counterbalanced by knowledge of the more
practical, if limited, achievements of his Anglo-Saxon predecessors, Wilfrid and Willibrord, nearer home.

It was Wilfrid's meteoric incursion into the continental
mission field in his Frisian campaign of 678–9 which first
kindled the missionary flame in Anglo-Saxon England, and
the example was never forgotten. Frisia was also the scene
of the more recent and more fruitful evangelism of Wilfrid's
pupil, Willibrord. To Frisia then, Winfrith would go, to
offer his services to Willibrord, to aid him in effecting the
conversion of the heathen tribes situated beyond the limits
of Frankish influence and protection, and to help reap the
ripening harvest of souls that Willibrord and his fellow-
labourers had sown.

Frisia (or Friesland), the scene of Winfrith's initiation
into the mission field, occupied at this time a key position in
Western Christendom. Territorially, it was equated with the
north-eastern provinces of modern Holland; politically, it
marked the limit of Frankish expansion to the east; eccle-
siastically, it formed a bridgehead for the advance of
Christianity into Saxony and North Germany. Throughout
its chequered history in the eighth century the fortunes of
the Christian mission rise or fall in direct proportion to the
strength or weakness of the Frankish state. As Levison
wrote, "Frankish dominion and Christian mission assisted
each other". The country was inhabited by warlike barbarians of Teutonic race akin to the Old Saxons and like
them deeply attached to their ancestral pagan worship. The
first penetration of the heathen crust had been effected by
Wilfrid of Ripon, who spent a whole winter there (678–9)
preaching and making converts. Many of the local chieftains
and hundreds of their followers were baptised, but nothing
was done to establish a church or organise a ministry. In

consequence most of Wilfrid's converts lapsed into paganism after his departure, despite the sporadic efforts of sundry wandering Irish preachers. The chief obstacle was the inveterate hostility of Radbod, the Frisian overlord, who was suspicious of the new religion as an instrument of Frankish aggression. So the situation remained in suspense until 690 when Willibrord of Northumbria, monk of Ripon and Wilfrid's pupil, arrived to take up the work where his master and the Irish monks had left it. Conditions appeared favourable to further progress. Radbod was being hard-pressed by Pippin of Heristal, the Frankish Mayor of the Palace and the real ruler of the kingdom. Pippin was determined to restore the Frankish frontier to its previous limits. Willibrord paid two visits to Rome, in 691 and 695, to awaken the interest of the pope and to obtain his support for the enterprise. On his second visit Pope Sergius consecrated him archbishop, conferred on him the pallium and gave him the Roman name of Clement. The work of building up the Frisian Church now began in earnest. Utrecht became Willibrord's archiepiscopal see. Several bishops were consecrated and attempts were made to train a native priesthood. Many Anglo-Saxon monks and clerks came over from England to participate in the work and a veritable English colony sprang up overseas. All these developments were promising enough, but Frisian Christianity was not yet firmly founded. From time to time there were setbacks and disappointments, marked by persecutions, apostasies and martyrdoms. So much depended on the exigencies of the political situation and on the support of Frankish arms. The disputed succession to the Frankish mayoralty, which ensued on the death of Pippin in 714 and only ended with the rise of Charles Martel in 719, had grave repercussions in Frisia. The Frankish garrisons were temporarily weakened and Radbod chose this moment to launch a war for the liberation of his people from the Frankish yoke and the extermination of Christianity, the faith of the foreign

conqueror. The insurrection put an end to the further progress of the mission, and Willibrord was forced to take
refuge in the monastery he had founded at Echternach.
This sudden and unexpected turn in events occurred at the
very time Winfrith in England was planning his venture.
He obviously had no inkling of the grave situation he would
have to face.

We do not know when, or in what circumstances, the call
to the Continent first came to Winfrith. Probably in his case
the sense of vocation was of gradual growth. At first, says
Willibald, he kept his hopes and ambitions to himself, but
later he opened them to Abbot Winbert, seeking his advice
and requesting his permission to go. The abbot at first gave
a peremptory refusal. Doubtless he was loth to lose a monk
so conspicuous as a scholar, a teacher and a priest, and
whose ability and integrity commanded respect throughout
ecclesiastical circles in Wessex. On the other hand, the repu-
tation of the abbey would be considerably enhanced if
Winfrith were to make good in his apostolate. Nursling
would then have its Willibrord, and Wessex its Wilfrid.
After the first rebuff Winfrith continued to press his suit
with such ardour and obstinacy that Abbot Winbert finally
gave way. The monks supplied him with money and ample
provisions for the journey. The abbot did more: he gave
permission for two or three of the brethren, whose hearts
had been fired by Winfrith's zeal, to accompany him and
share the perils and hardships of his lot. So, fortified by the
benediction of the abbot and the prayers of the brethren,
the little band set out for the Continent, probably in the
spring of 716. They embarked at London in a Frisian ship
and crossed to Dorstadt, an inland port on the River Lek
about twelve miles south of Utrecht, the headquarters of
Willibrord's mission. Here their astonished eyes beheld the
ruin of their hopes. The situation was far worse than reports
had led them to expect. Willibrord had gone into exile and
there were no responsible leaders left among the Frisian

Christians. Radbod was laying waste the whole country-side with fire and sword, adopting "a scorched earth" policy in his campaign against the Franks. Everywhere he was ruthlessly destroying churches and monasteries, renovating pagan shrines and temples and restoring their worship. The Frisian Church had apparently been annihilated and Frisian Christianity, where it still existed, had been driven underground. Winfrith did what he could to retrieve the situation. He succeeded in gaining an interview with Radbod in Utrecht, but the heathen champion refused to listen to his plea, to grant him leave to preach freely or to make any concessions in mitigation of the persecution. For some months Winfrith persevered in his uphill task, but he found all roads closed to him in "this sterile land", as Willibald calls it. At last, either in the autumn of 716 or in the spring of 717, he resigned himself to the failure of his enterprise and decided to return to England. Nothing tangible had been gained, nothing salvaged from the ruins, no contact had been established with the absent Willibrord; the expedition seemed outwardly a complete fiasco. Yet there was something to be placed on the credit side of the account. Winfrith had learnt much from his almost literal baptism of fire on the mission front. He had come to realise that zeal and enthusiasm were not enough to guarantee success. Training, planning and organisation were equally essential. How well he learnt this lesson the story of his German mission will unfold. The time was long since past when free-lance preachers of the Irish type could hope to achieve lasting results. Conditions on the Continent were slowly changing, and the task of an evangelist was becoming harder rather than easier. Strong and consistent support from the ecclesiastical hierarchy, no less than from the secular government of the Frankish state, was an indispensable guarantee of permanent success. In any future venture he must be sure of his ground, and his status as a preacher of the gospel among the heathen would need to be sanctioned and fortified by the highest ecclesiastical authority. For Winfrith returned to England undaunted by his failure in Frisia and more than ever certain of his calling. His first ill-fated adventure may be regarded, in Kurth's happy phrase, as a "journey on reconnaissance". Next time it would be the real thing, and there would be no turning back.

Home again at Nursling, he resumed his old life of teaching and priestly ministration in the abbey. His failure abroad had in no wise diminished his prestige at home or the respect and affection in which he was held there. For when Abbot Winbert, now grown old and feeble, died a year or more later, Winfrith was unanimously elected as his successor. But his mind was fully made up. He was already planning a second voyage overseas. He therefore refused the office of abbot. He informed his diocesan, Daniel of Winchester, of the grounds of his refusal, and solicited his good offices with the monks. Daniel was an understanding bishop. He not only accepted Winfrith's excuses and himself provided a suitable candidate for the vacancy, but he warmly encouraged him in his project and furnished him with two letters of recommendation for his journey. The first (*Ep.* 11) was a general letter entreating all secular and ecclesiastical princes, whose lands he might traverse, to extend him hospitality; the second was a letter of introduction to the pope. For Winfrith had resolved to make Rome his first objective. He would acquaint the pope with his plans, seek counsel and blessing from the Holy Father and place himself at his command. The pope should decide in what corner of Christ's vineyard he should be set to work. If his services were accepted, he would from henceforth appear as the accredited representative of the Vicar of Christ. Such ideas were part of the normal Anglo-Saxon religious tradition. The English Church was the child of Rome, founded by Pope Gregory the Great through the agency of St Augustine and bound ever since to the Apostolic See by the strongest ties of gratitude, loyalty and obedience. In this respect

Winfrith was no innovator. Willibrord in his time had sought counsel, inspiration and authority from Rome, and it is more than likely that Bishop Daniel encouraged Winfrith to follow this example.

Fortified by Daniel's letter he set out on the long and hazardous trek to Rome, probably in the late autumn of 718. This time he crossed the Channel as one of a band of pilgrims. He was destined never to set foot in England again. The little company reached the Holy City in safety, gave thanks to God and made offerings at St Peter's tomb. A week or two later Winfrith had his first audience with the pope. Gregory II, who then occupied the papal chair, was a man of character and intelligence, experienced in statecraft and gifted with political insight above the average, a good judge of men, and altogether a worthy successor of the great pope whose name he bore. At the interview he treated his visitor with courtesy and tact, listening patiently while Winfrith explained the reasons for his coming and confided to him his cherished ambitions. The pope gazed at him "with cheerful countenance and smiling eyes" and inquired whether he had brought any letter of introduction from his bishop. Winfrith then produced Daniel's letter, which the pope perused without further comment. This was the first of many interviews and many intimate talks between the two men, but the details of their conversation are not recorded. Gregory was in no hurry to make up his mind, and he kept Winfrith waiting in Rome for the rest of the winter. Hauck rightly draws attention to the importance of the length of his sojourn there. Frequent interchange of ideas engendered mutual confidence between the two men, and this was a powerful contribution to success in the early stages of the German mission. At last, in the early summer of 719, Gregory took a decisive step. He was not yet quite sure of his man: he would put him to the proof. He would send him on an exploratory mission to Thuringia, the region of Germany lying far to the east of the Rhine,

between the forest of that name in the south and the Harz
mountains in the north. Here he could operate with a roving
commission under the specific authority of the Apostolic
See. For Gregory had long been planning a new drive into
central Germany, where the first fruits of the wandering
Irish preachers were still waiting to be gathered in.

The formal mandate (*Ep.* 12) commissioning Winfrith as
a missionary under the direct authority of the pope is dated
15th May, 719. It is addressed "to the devout priest,
Boniface". This is the first mention of Winfrith's new name,
and there is no doubt that it was bestowed on him then in
honour of the Roman martyr whose feast was kept the day
before, and not, subsequently in 722, on the occasion of his
consecration as bishop, as Willibald erroneously states. Confirmation of the earlier date is given in his collected correspondence where, in letters manifestly written to him before
722, he is addressed as Boniface. He used the new name
consistently throughout the remainder of his life, and under
it his career has been immortalised and his memory hallowed. In all probability Gregory II was consciously following the precedent set by Pope Sergius when he renamed
Willibrord Clement in 695. It is noteworthy that the papal
mandate is couched in the vaguest terms. It contains no
mention of Thuringia, or even of Germany, and no specific
definition of the scope and nature of Boniface's activities.
He is commissioned to preach the gospel "in heathen parts"
and to administer the sacraments according to the rites and
formularies of the Apostolic See, to whom he is to refer all
difficulties and necessities that may arise. Although his new
rôle remained unclarified in the papal mandate, Boniface
well understood the pope's mind. He was to go to Germany
and set up his headquarters in Thuringia. He had been
given a new name and a new country, a new lease of life in
the pope's service. In one sense it constituted a break with
the past, of which the change of name was a fitting symbol.

About midsummer in 719 he took his departure from

Rome carrying with him the pope's blessing on his future labours. Crossing the Alps, he passed through Bavaria, and entered Thuringia, where the Irish missionaries had hitherto had the field to themselves. For all that, he found the religion of the natives in a bad way. Paganism had begun to rear its ugly head again, and to infiltrate into Christianity. All sorts of strange ideas and superstitions were current among both priests and laity, and where a purer form of Christianity survived, it invariably conformed to the Celtic usages and customs. Willibald, in the saint's biography, makes mention of corrupt and evil clerks who degraded their Christian profession by participation in the idolatrous rites of Thor and Woden. Boniface was to experience a deal of trouble from men of this character throughout his career as an evangelist. In this particular case he strove to recall them by argument and exhortation to purity of doctrine and righteousness of life. But he apparently made little headway, and he found his position invidious and anomalous, since most of the leaders did not recognise the authority of the pope. He therefore judged it prudent to enlist the support of Charles Martel and the Frankish bishops in the hope of obtaining reinforcements from the Frankish monks and clergy. Accordingly he set out for Charles' court, but he never reached it. On the way he received tidings of a remarkable change in the situation in Frisia. Radbod, the stout-hearted pagan warrior, was dead, the Frankish army had regained control. Willibrord was back in Utrecht, preaching, planning and organising the Frisian Church of the future. Boniface decided to postpone his visit to the Frankish court, and instead took ship down the Rhine to Utrecht in order to join forces with Willibrord. This abrupt change of plan need occasion no surprise. He had not been irrevocably committed by the papal mandate to any one sphere of operations. It had certainly been Gregory II's intention that he should make Thuringia the venue of his "tour of inspection", as Willibald calls it, but he had been

given a roving commission as an itinerant preacher in the
pope's service, and he therefore felt justified in transferring
his activities back to the scene of his early labours. For the
time being, he judged, he could best serve the Christian
cause and the papal interests by acting as Willibrord's
lieutenant.

Thus began three years (719–22) of fruitful collaboration
between the two great Anglo-Saxon missionaries. They
formed a perfect combination for the task. Archbishop
Willibrord was now over sixty years of age, and his last
twenty years had been spent in the Frisian mission field. He
was a master of the missionary technique, but by now somewhat lacking in the drive and energy needed for the recon-
struction of an ordered Christian society out of the ruins of
the past six years. These qualities Boniface, still in his middle
forties, could amply supply. If he learned much from the
older man, he gave something of value in return. In Frisia
he first displayed that consummate ability for planning and
organisation which was to be a distinctive feature of his
work in Germany in later years. He was more than Willibrord's lieutenant; he was his right-hand man. Moreover, his
presence and participation in the common enterprise was an
earnest of the approval and support of the Papacy. We have
no detailed information concerning their joint labours, but it
is clear that the net result was the establishment of a provincial church in western or Frankish Frisia on firm foundations, the eastern and barbarian half of the country remaining still untouched. In more concrete terms this meant the
destruction of pagan shrines and temples and the enforced
cessation of pagan worship, the rebuilding of derelict
churches and monasteries and the construction of new ones,
the reconciliation of the weaker brethren who had lapsed
under the strain of persecution, the training of priests and
teachers for the conversion of multitudes still ignorant of the
gospel message, the subjection of both monks and secular
clergy to the discipline of the canonical life, and the crea-

tion of administrative machinery suited to the special conditions of the mission field by the consecration of "country-bishops" (*chorepiscopi*), an expedient which Boniface was to adopt later in Hesse and Thuringia. Willibrord was desperately anxious to keep Boniface with him in Frisia permanently. He looked on him as his natural successor as head of the mission in the event of his own death or incapacity for duty through advancing age and infirmity. He therefore proposed to consecrate him as bishop-coadjutor in the diocese of Utrecht, but Boniface incontinently refused to accept the office. He pleaded his personal unworthiness, his comparative inexperience and the fact that he had not yet reached the canonical age of fifty, though this would not have constituted an insuperable obstacle. He remained deaf to all Willibrord's entreaties and unconvinced by his arguments. At last he brought forward the papal mandate of 719 to justify his refusal. The pope had commissioned him to preach among the heathen at large. He could only obtain his release and permission to undertake the office of a bishop from the pope in person. To this Willibrord had no answer. Sorrowfully he was forced to abandon his cherished scheme and allow Boniface to depart. The two men parted as friends and with full understanding of each other's point of view; Willibrord to sustain the increasingly heavy burden of his office till death overtook him seventeen years later (739); Boniface, with the archbishop's blessing, to begin his work in Hesse. Thus ended a notable partnership which redounds to the credit of the Anglo-Saxon race.

Hesse, the scene of Boniface's new activities, was the region bordering Thuringia on its western flank and lying between the upper reaches of the Weser and the waters of the middle Rhine. It was a frontier province of the Frankish kingdom of Austrasia, but the writ of the Austrasian king only ran when and where there were Frankish garrisons to enforce it. It was a wild and primitive country, intersected by mountain ranges and covered with dense, primeval

forests, where Woden, Thor and the other deities of the
Teutonic pantheon might well seem alive and all-powerful
to the tribal warrior who inhabited it. Christianity had, as
it were, passed over the land with the itinerant Celtic
preachers, but it had never lingered or taken root there, and
the mass of the people were sunk in the superstitions and
cruelties of their ancestral pagan worship. It formed a
heathen pocket in the Thuringian mission field, for it had
been utterly neglected by the Frankish bishops of Mainz
within whose diocese it lay. For all that, it was a strategic
point for the drive into central Germany. Here was virgin
soil for a Catholic evangelist working under papal auspices.
Here was a task calculated to try Boniface's mettle to the
uttermost, as Gregory II had doubtless intended it should.
Hesse was the real beginning of his apostolate, the scene of
his greatest travails and also, as we shall see, of his most
spectacular triumph. In Thuringia, at his first coming in
719, he had found centres of Christianity and a rudimen-
tary church organisation already in existence. In Hesse he
enjoyed no such initial advantages. Here he had to start
from scratch, employing the technique he had learnt from
Willibrord in Frisia during the years of his apprenticeship.
He began with the chieftains. At Amöneburg on the river
Ohm, seven miles east of Marburg, he succeeded in con-
verting two of them, twin brothers named Dettic and
Deorulf, and soon acquired a substantial following among
the local tribesmen. Here he built a small, rude chapel for
worship, on the site of which was later reared a splendid
monastery, the first of his many foundations. It was a
promising start, and from here the work moved steadily
forward. "Thousands", Willibald tells us with patent ex-
aggeration, were weaned from the practice of pagan
idolatry and baptized into the Christian faith. A like success attended his efforts in other tribal centres, but his little
band of preachers and helpers was all too small for the
magnitude of the task he had set himself. He needed recruits,

and quickly too. He needed counsel and moral support from the pope and the Frankish hierarchy. It was high time that he got into touch with Rome again. So he despatched one of his disciples, named Binna, to Rome to report progress to Gregory II. The messenger carried with him a letter giving the pope a detailed account of what had so far been accomplished and seeking guidance from him on certain difficult problems of conduct and procedure peculiar to the mission field. The pope's answer, which Binna delivered on his return, contained a summons to Rome for further consultation. Boniface promptly and joyfully obeyed.

Accompanied by a select band of disciples he set out on his second visit to the Holy City. He took a circuitous route through Frankish and Burgundian territory before crossing the Alps and making his way through Lombardy to reach Rome early in November 722. The pope received him in audience at St Peter's. He was well satisfied with Boniface's record of the past three years. His initial successes in Thuringia and Hesse had exceeded expectations. He had proved himself worthy of promotion to a higher rank entailing heavier responsibilities. Gregory had decided to make him a bishop. But first he must be absolutely sure of his orthodoxy, in conformity with the canons. He therefore began by interrogating him concerning his doctrine and teaching. Boniface at first showed some hesitation and embarrassment. Where such grave theological truths were in question, he doubtless found it difficult to give, verbally and all unprepared, a clear and succinct exposition of his faith. Moreover, as a foreigner, trained to think and speak in the classical Latin of the schools, he was hard put to it to understand the vulgar and provincial Latin which the pope spoke. He therefore begged for a few days' grace in order to set down his beliefs in writing. To this the pope agreed, and Boniface duly presented his profession of faith, "written in polished and eloquent Latin", a day or two later.

Within a week Gregory summoned him to a second

C

audience in the Lateran. Wholly reassured as to his orthodoxy, the pope took him into his confidence, and the two
men spent nearly all day reviewing the many problems and
needs of the German mission field. Finally the pope an-
nounced his intention to consecrate him bishop. This time
there could be no refusal. Boniface dared not question the
decision of the Apostolic Vicar. Humbly and obediently he
accepted the onerous office. He was to be consecrated
bishop for all Germany east of the Rhine, but without
episcopal seat and owing obedience to no metropolitan, but
solely to the pope. He was consecrated in Rome on the feast
of St Andrew (30th November 722), a highly appropriate
day, for, like the Apostle, he was called to be a "fisher of
men". At his consecration he took an oath of loyalty and
obedience to the Apostolic See. This has been the subject of
needless misunderstanding and much unfavourable comment. There was nothing novel, peculiar or gratuitous in his
action. He was merely conforming to the established
practice of Italian prelates at their consecration, and the
text of the oath, which has come down to us, follows the
usual form subscribed by the suburbicarian bishops of the
Roman Church with one important modification. The
clause promising allegiance to the Byzantine Emperor at
Constantinople as the successor of the Roman Emperor of
the West, which would have been altogether pointless for a
Frankish or German bishop, was replaced by a clause binding the newly consecrated prelate to hold no communion or
fellowship with bishops who did not obey the canons of the
Roman Church or the traditions of the Fathers, to oppose
them to the utmost of his power and to report all such cases
to the pope. This alteration was dictated by common prudence in the light of the conditions obtaining in the German
mission field. It was designed primarily to guard against the
dissemination of heresy and false teaching among the
Hessian and Thuringian Christians by the errant—and
sometimes erring—Irish preachers whom Boniface would

frequently encounter in the discharge of his episcopal functions. It was also intended to cover his relations with the
corrupt and worldly Frankish bishops. But though there is
nothing novel or sinister about the terms of the oath, the
fact that it was taken is undoubtedly of cardinal importance.
It opened new and closer relations with the Roman See. It
bound him to the pope in a special way. By it he was
charged to act as the papal representative in the wider
sphere of Christian politics and statecraft. He was to be, not
only a bishop and an evangelist, but also virtually papal
commissioner in Germany. From the letters which Gregory
wrote on his behalf early in December 722, addressed to the
Christian chieftains and their people in Thuringia (*Epp.* 18,
19) and to "the glorious Duke Charles" (*Ep.* 20), there
is every indication that he was planning the integration of
the Christian converts of Hesse and Thuringia into a provincial church under the direct authority and supervision of
the pope.

Early in the following year Boniface was on his way back
to Germany. Again he took the longer route through
Frankish territory. His purpose in so doing was to visit
Charles Martel, to deliver the pope's letter to him and to
reinforce it with a personal plea for Charles's goodwill and
support for the task the pope had laid upon him. Charles
was by no means single-minded in his devotion to the
Church or actuated by filial piety towards the Apostolic
See. He was a man of action who had had to fight hard to
win supreme power in the Frankish realm, a fierce and ruth-
less warrior, with a good deal of the barbarian in him below
the surface. His ecclesiastical policy was forthright and independent. He was determined to rule the Frankish Church in
his own way, and to exploit it if he thought fit. He was no
friend to clerks and monks, and his sequestration of ecclesiastical estates in order to provide lands and revenues for his
Frankish warriors and so increase the war potential of the
nation, had incurred suspicion and hostility at Rome. But,

as the actual ruler of the Frankish kingdom and the chief
Catholic power of the West, his support for the eastward
expansion of Christendom and his protection of the Anglo-
Saxon missionaries engaged in the enterprise, would be invaluable, even indispensable. The success of the venture,
moreover, would be to Charles' own interests. Hesse and
Thuringia constituted frontier provinces of the Frankish
dominions, springboards for the extension of Frankish power
into heathen and barbarian Saxony, from which came
always the chief threat to the peace and security of Austrasia. Charles was nothing if not a realist. Political con-
siderations alone dictated a policy of understanding and
friendship with the pope and at least a show of co-operation
with Boniface and his fellows. Accordingly he issued a formal
mandate (*Ep.* 22) commending Boniface and his cause to all
Frankish officials and ordering them to grant him safe-
conduct and protection throughout his dominions. It is
significant that the letter makes no mention of the pope or
of the fact that Boniface had come to Charles as papal
envoy. Boniface is treated as a Frankish bishop who has
been granted facilities for a special task approved by the
Frankish government.

Once this privilege had been secured, Boniface hastened
his return to Hesse. There things had not gone too well during his absence of nearly a year. Some of his early converts
had relapsed into paganism. Others were trying "to make
the best of both worlds", professing openly to be Christians,
but secretly participating in the nocturnal orgies of the old
religion. Yet others, of stouter heart and nobler metal, were
holding fast to Christ in face of unpopularity and persecution. The return of their leader rallied the waverers and
consolidated the Christian forces. There were gains to be
registered as well as losses. The disciples of Boniface had
made new converts during his absence, and his first act as
bishop was to administer the sacrament of confirmation to
those of his own converts who had remained true to their

baptismal vows and to those who had recently been brought into the fold. But there was a great deal more to be done, if the gospel was to make real progress. He had not yet bitten into the core of Teutonic heathenism. All around him was tangible evidence that Hessian paganism was in a mighty flourishing state; the sacred groves, the holy mountains, the streams and springs and waterfalls, each the chosen habitation of some nature-god or goddess, each with its shrine or altar served by priestly clans and adored by thousands of worshippers: all this dark primeval world of superstition, idolatry and cruelty was pulsating with life and energy. Boniface decided on a bold stroke. He would strike at the very heart of this religion of evil, and he would do so in circumstances which would either bring complete and final victory to the cause of Christ or win for him a martyr's crown. He would cause the whole body of neighbouring tribesmen to be summoned as to a tribal moot, and in full view of the assembled multitude, friends and foes alike, he would cut down the giant oak of Geismar, the sacred tree dedicated to Thor from time immemorial, the chief centre of the cult of the Thunder-god in all Germany. It was the most spectacular and dramatic event of his whole life, and has kindled the imagination of posterity like none other of his achievements. As Willibald tells the story, simply (for once!) and without excess or elaboration, we can easily conjure up the scene. The gigantic tree, full grown in majesty and splendour, deep in the oak forest half-way up the mountain side, a living witness to the faith of their ancestors; the Christian priest, advancing axe in hand, supported by his small band of devoted disciples and a numerous body of native Christians, while a horde of heathen warriors pressed silently but menacingly round them waiting for the Thunderer to avenge this sacrilegious violation of his sanctuary with one bolt from his celestial armoury. The intrepid bishop closed in on his objective. Still the Thunderer remained mute, even when the first dread blow of the axe fell.

The whole tree shivered at the stroke, and a sudden powerful gust of wind snapped the topmost branches. Calmly, inexorably the saintly woodman worked on—Boniface must have been skilled in woodcraft—raining blow after blow of the axe upon the gnarled and massive trunk, till at last with a mighty crash the giant monster fell, its trunk bursting asunder into four parts which, as they fell to the ground, miraculously shaped themselves into the arms of a cross, each arm of equal length. The struggle was over, Christ, through his doughty champion, had vindicated his people. The crowd dissolved amid a Babel of voices. The discomfited heathen warriors, who had come to curse and blaspheme, returned home to bless and praise Christ, says Willibald. Boniface used the timber of the fallen oak to construct a rude and simple chapel, dedicated to St Peter, in commemoration of the event. On or near the spot in after years rose the monastery of Fritzlar. The destruction of Thor's oak broke the back of pagan resistance in Hesse. The preaching of the gospel now went forward with certainty of ultimate success. The victory of Geismar had come at the psychological moment, when many of the tribesmen were wavering in their allegiance to the old religion and secretly hoping for a convenient opportunity to declare in favour of the new. It is worthy of note that Willibald expressly states that Boniface took the decisive step on the advice of the Hessian Christians, who were presumably aware of the trend in popular opinion and accurately weighed the chances of success. Schmidt regards the incident as a demonstration of Boniface's "consummate tactics". He timed his assault at exactly the right moment. Statesmanship, no less than courage, contributed to achieve the desired result. Perhaps after all the real drama of Geismar was enacted in the realm of the mind and the spirit.

But there were many obstacles to be overcome before the fruits of victory could be safely gathered in. There were other pagan shrines to be demolished and other Teutonic deities to be dethroned before the Christian Faith could be propagated without let or hindrance. From Willibald's narrative we get the impression that Boniface, flushed with his triumph at Geismar, pressed on to neighbouring Thuringia, the scene of his brief exploratory mission of 719, but this is by no means certain. Two letters in the saint's correspondence throw light upon his activities at this time, and their contents apply equally well to the situation in Hesse and to that in Thuringia. The first is from Boniface's friend and former diocesan, Daniel, bishop of Winchester (*Ep.* 23) and was written in 723 or 724 in answer to one from Boniface no longer extant, in which apparently he had asked Daniel's advice on the best methods to be employed in the conversion of the heathen. Daniel's letter is marked by sound commonsense and not a little insight, though it is somewhat patronising in tone and savours a little of "armchair criticism". He counsels caution and moderation in the further stages of the campaign. The heathen should be converted by persuasion and argument rather than by violence and intimidation. If, as is not impossible, Daniel had already heard of the Geismar exploit, it would seem that he mistrusted the efficacy of such flamboyant and spectacular methods. If Boniface was perhaps disappointed with this letter, he can have derived nothing but pleasure and encouragement from another received from Pope Gregory II (*Ep.* 24) at the close of 724 in reply to a confidential report on the progress of the mission sent to Rome the previous year. Boniface has made an excellent beginning, the pope writes in effect, but this is no time for resting on his oars. Let him not slacken in the sacred enterprise. Salvation is promised to him who endures to the end. So long as the will is steadfast, God will crown his struggle with victory. Let him cease not to preach the word "in season and out of season". Boniface had complained to the pope about the obstructive tactics of the Frankish bishops, particularly Gerold of Mainz, who was doing his utmost to thwart the progress of the mission in Thuringia while claiming that the region came under his episcopal jurisdiction. In his reply the pope states that he has written to Charles Martel about the bishop, and he can safely be left to the Frankish ruler for appropriate action.

These two letters, in combination with Willibald's narrative, give some idea of the confused and disordered scene in Hesse and Thuringia. Boniface encountered obstacles at every turn; problems natural to the conditions of the mission field in any age, and those arising from the peculiar political situation in Germany and the Frankish kingdom. All seemed equally urgent for solution. Boniface and his little band of devoted helpers might well be pardoned for flinching at the magnitude of their task. How were the canons of the Church on law and morals to be applied to tribal communities where barbarism was of hoary antiquity and Christianity was new or nascent? What was the proper procedure in cases where the administration of the sacraments of baptism and confirmation had been negligent, irregular or defective? Were these sacraments valid and canonical when performed by Irish monk-missionaries or itinerant priests whose claim to be bishops had no foundation? Should the sacramental rite be repeated where there was any lingering doubt or suspicion? Should the penitential system of the Church be applied in its full rigour in cases of apostasy or breach of baptismal vows when, as so often, there were extenuating circumstances? What line ought to be taken in dealing with "mixed marriages" between Christians and pagans, and how strictly or leniently should the prohibited degrees of consanguinity be enforced in a barbarous community where marriage between kinsfolk was the normal custom? Should those who had entered the "religious" life in childhood be permitted as adults to quit the cloister in order to marry? What was the best way of dealing with pagan superstitions where they had been carried over into Christian life and practice? Were Boniface and his brethren justified in remaining in communion with priests and clerks notorious for their evil lives or suspect of heresy, and in sharing with them the common meal? Such questions, and a hundred and one others, some of grave import and involving cardinal principles, others of minor significance, or even trivial to our modern way of thinking, but all of them daily encountered in his pastoral ministration, grievously oppressed the mind and conscience of Boniface at this crucial time. Here in Thuringia he had to solve problems emanating from conditions far more barbarous, confused and complex, than those he had experienced in his work with Willibrord in Frisia five or six years earlier. By 726 he had come to feel the imperative necessity of seeking guidance from Rome. Accordingly that same year he dispatched to the pope a *questionnaire* on these and other burning topics. It was carried to Rome by a messenger named Denuald, who may almost certainly be identified with the Denehard who was prominent among the saint's early disciples. The particular points, instanced above, on which Boniface sought the pope's guidance have been deduced from the latter's reply (*Ep*. 26) dated 22nd November 726. Gregory's answers are clear and succinct, and have the full force of the Roman canons behind them. Another link, of a moral and spiritual kind, had been forged between Rome and the nascent Christianity of central Germany.

But these were not the only obstacles Boniface had to surmount. There were others engendered by unstable social and political conditions. Thuringia was a barren and poverty-stricken land, subject to frequent ravages at the hands of the wild and heathen Saxons. From time to time some tiny and ill-defended Christian outpost would be overrun, its inhabitants exterminated, or a few wretched survivors compelled to flee for their very lives. Eighth century Germany, no less than the twentieth, had its refugee problem. Such ruin and desolation involved setbacks to the work of spreading the gospel. Frequently Boniface had to

turn from the task of preaching the word of God and building churches to that of providing succour and defence of a
purely material kind for his Christian converts. There was
more than enough to discourage even the stoutest-hearted
evangelist: the obduracy of pagan chieftains; the treachery
and cruelty of Christian Frankish governors and officials;
the dissemination of heresy and false teaching by wandering
preachers of the Celtic school, whose activities were detrimental to the ordered and disciplined church life Boniface
was striving to inculcate. To make matters worse, Boniface
had lost touch with Charles Martel on whom he depended
for the protection of his mission. Charles was interpreting
his obligations in a negative or minimal sense, while
Boniface had hoped for more positive action from the mandate of 723. This lack of contact and understanding with the
Frankish government was a definite disadvantage to Boniface
in the political sphere, though it certainly gave him a freer
hand in ecclesiastical administration and enabled him to
avoid embarrassing relations with the corrupt and worldly
Frankish hierarchy. Then, too, the shortage of man-power
was becoming more acute with the expansion of the
mission. Whence was he to obtain reinforcements for his
spiritual warfare against the powers of evil, ignorance and
superstition? Priests and monks, lay preachers and experts
in education, nuns and women workers; all were in great
demand. He sent out appeals throughout Western Christendom. The response from the Frankish realm was meagre and
disappointing; the response from his native land was mag-
nificent and overwhelming. Boniface was still a living
memory in the Anglo-Saxon world. His friends and kinsfolk
in Wessex had not forgotten him during his long sojourn
abroad. With some of them he had contrived, despite his
busy life as a man of action, to carry on a fitful correspondence, and it was primarily through such epistolary contacts that he succeeded in maintaining the interest and enthusiasm of Anglo-Saxon churchmen for the German

mission at fever pitch. The movement of Anglo-Saxon
"religious colonisation" in central Germany, as it may be
called, began with a trickle of helpers from Wessex. By 732
the trickle had become a flowing stream; by 746 it had
swollen to a flood. Willibald tells us that the first band of
ardent disciples contained "readers and writers and learned
men trained in the other arts". Some of them were already
monks, and others now placed themselves under the Benedictine Rule at the instigation of Boniface. Some were put
to work in scattered groups in Hesse, others in Thuringia,
spreading the knowledge of the gospel in towns and villages
in ever widening circles. Othlo, monk of St. Emmeram near
Ratisbon, an eleventh century biographer, who added considerably to the material used by Willibald, corroborates
this and gives the names of some of the men and women
from England who answered the call. Among the first to
join Boniface in Germany were Wigbert, a monk of Glastonbury, who became the first abbot of Fritzlar; Burchard, a
monk of Malmesbury, who was set to work in Thuringia and
was later made bishop of Wurzburg; the priest Denehard,
so often employed on confidential embassies to Rome; Lull,
another Malmesbury monk and probably also a former
pupil of Boniface at Nursling, who was to succeed his master
as the head of the mission and in the see of Mainz; the
brothers Willibald (not the biographer) and Winnebald,
the saint's distant cousins, who by devious routes and diverse
experiences had both been drawn into the apostolic charmed
circle. Some were powerful preachers, others were finished
scholars or skilled administrators. All were trained for their
special tasks in the hard school of the German mission field
under the vigilant eye and loving care of the master-builder.
Nor must the galaxy of nuns and noble women be forgotten,
though most of these arrived in Germany at a later date,
probably not much before 746. Among them were Cunihild,
the maternal aunt of Lull, who, with her daughter Bergit
(or Bertha), worked as teachers among women in Thuringia;

they are described as "learned in the liberal arts";
Cunitrude, put to a similar task in Bavaria; Walpurgis, the
sister of Willibald and Winnebald, who became abbess of
Heidenheim and a legendary figure in medieval German
folklore, and finally the saint's two female relatives, Thecla,
who presided successively over the nunneries of Kitzingen
and Ochsenfurt, and the unique and admirable Lioba (or
Leofgyth), the brightest star in this fair constellation and the
best beloved in Christ among Boniface's women helpers.
Lioba became abbess of the double monastery of Tauberbischofsheim, some thirty miles from Wurzburg, and was
closely associated with Boniface during the closing years of
his life. We shall meet her and some of the others again in
connection with Boniface's personal friendships and his
correspondence. To the dedicated lives and heroic self-
sacrifice of such men and women the spiritual and cultural
progress of the native Christians of central Germany was
chiefly due. "The Christian culture", wrote Hauck, "which
they had so happily unfolded in England they brought over
with them to Germany."

In spite of all the difficulties and setbacks the work of
Christianising the heathen communities in Hesse and Thuringia went forward after 725 by leaps and bounds. The
drive and initiative of Boniface, the zeal and enthusiasm of
his growing band of workers and the wise counsel and
staunch support of Pope Gregory II were the main reasons
for the astonishing progress made in the following decade.
Progress was to be measured, not solely or chiefly by the
host of converts made—on several occasions mass-baptisms of
hundreds, even thousands, of tribesmen took place—but
still more by the building of churches and chapels, schools
and monasteries, hallowing acre after acre of barbarian
territory for Christ. In Boniface's opinion monasteries had a
vital part to play in the barbarian mission field, and there
is no doubt that he was right. A monastery was not only a
centre of prayer and worship, a "spiritual power-house",

but it was also a centre of learning and instruction, where the native Christian population could learn the rudiments of social order as well as of religious faith. As Kurth finely wrote, "Every (monastic) foundation of Boniface was a conquest of barbarian soil necessarily to be made before he could achieve the conquest of barbarian hearts." Amidst the trail of ruin and desolation left by Saxon forays and the punitive operations of Frankish armies the monasteries kept burning the lamps of civilisation and radiated the spirit of Christian peace and charity. They were in a literal sense the *seminaries* or seed-plots of the Christian Faith. Besides Amöneburg and Fritzlar already mentioned, another house was built at Ohrdruf, just beyond the northern fringe of the Thuringian Forest. Three houses for women followed, the counterparts of the older foundations for monks. In a few years Hesse and Thuringia were sprinkled with centres of the "religious" life, and by 732 Boniface was able to reap the fruits of his labours in rich abundance. A native provincial church had been firmly established on Roman and Anglo-Saxon foundations, which in Hauck's considered view "surpassed all the provincial churches of the Frankish realm, both in religious and intellectual life."

The year 732 brought Boniface to another milestone. He had ably fulfilled the commission enjoined on him by Gregory II ten years earlier at his consecration as bishop, and in the course of doing so he had come to lean more and more on Rome. But the old pope did not live long enough to see the consummation of his policy or to recompense Boniface's signal services by some further honour or reward. In January 731 he had died in Rome. His successor was his namesake, Gregory III, destined to be a notable pope, a clear, bold and far-sighted statesman who shared his predecessor's enthusiasm for the expansion of Christendom and his sympathetic understanding of the tremendous issues involved. The change in the occupant of the papal chair thus made no immediate alteration in the wider field of

papal policy or in Boniface's personal relations with the
Holy See. Boniface sent a letter of formal greeting to the
new pope, assuring him of his loyalty and obedience and
soliciting the pope's favour and the maintenance of the
existing good understanding between the German mission
and Rome. He followed this up next year (732) with an
up-to-date and detailed report on the progress of his work.
To this Gregory replied in the course of that same year
(*Ep.* 28), congratulating Boniface on his successes and ap-
proving in general terms the measures taken to safeguard
the ground already won. In the same letter he announces
Boniface's elevation to the rank of archbishop and the
bestowal of the pallium as the insignia of his new office.
Further, he grants him permission to consecrate a limited
number of bishops from among his disciples to aid him in
the discharge of his pastoral duties. A new phase in the
history of the mission was thus opened, but it did not
materially alter Boniface's own position as an evangelist
working under papal auspices with a roving commission.
He was now to be a *regionary archbishop without a province*, but
with full metropolitan authority over all Germany east of
the Rhine, just as up till then he had been a *regionary bishop
without a see*. Nevertheless, the new situation thus created
was not entirely free from ambiguity, since, if he were to act
on the pope's permission to consecrate bishops, the step
might entail the partition of the Hessian and Thuringian
churches into a number of dioceses, and Boniface would
then find himself in an anomalous position without a metropolitan see. This is what actually happened in course of
time. Whether Boniface was conscious of the fact or not, it
is plain that the bestowal of the archbishop's pallium
marked a change not only in his ecclesiastical status, but
also in the nature of his activities. All the evidence goes to
show that he still thought of his task as primarily the
evangelisation of the heathen, and of himself as the leader
of a band of mission preachers. In these very years he was

contemplating the extension of his preaching among the heathen Saxons, whom he thought of as his "blood-brothers" and dearly hoped to win for Christ. He had even been thinking of resigning his office as a bishop in order to obtain greater freedom and leisure for that task. It was probably to clear up any misunderstanding and to obtain the pope's assent to this "self-denying ordinance" that Boniface paid his third visit to Rome in 738. If he had hoped to win over the pope, he was soon disillusioned. Gregory received him graciously, but disapproved of the Saxon project as being untimely. He flatly refused to accept his resignation, admonished him on his duty of filial obedience to the Holy See and sent him back to his post in Thuringia fortified with letters (*Epp.* 42, 43) commending him to all ranks of society as their archbishop. The pope went further. He enlarged Boniface's commission by laying upon him the task of reforming and reorganising the provincial churches in Bavaria and Allemannia. A papal rescript addressed to the bishops of those regions (*Ep.* 44) commands them to acknowledge the authority of Boniface as papal vicar and commissioner for all Germany and to render him full obedience. Boniface could do nothing but acquiesce in the pope's decision, and as a token of his complete and unswerving loyalty he renewed at this time his solemn oath of obedience to the Holy See. Thus opened a new and decisive chapter in his life's work, the "advance into Bavaria". There he was to find ample scope for the exercise of that talent for organisation and administration already manifest in his apostolate in Hesse and Thuringia. The keen eyes of Gregory III had discerned with unerring accuracy both the most pressing need of the German Church and the true genius of Boniface.

II. BONIFACE AS ECCLESIASTICAL
ORGANISER AND STATESMAN

The constructive achievements of St Boniface as an ecclesiastical organiser and statesman of the first rank have not until recent years received in his own country the attention they deserve. English historians in the past have tended to stress the prime importance of his career as the first Anglo-Saxon missionary to operate on a large scale on the continent of Europe and to depreciate the work of "building up the churches" of southern and central Germany, which he undertook at the command of Pope Gregory III in 738, and the cognate task of reforming the corrupt and decadent "Mother Church" of the Frankish realm to which he was summoned by Carloman and Pippin, the sons and successors of Charles Martel, in 742. This is perhaps only natural. To the average Englishman "the Apostle of Germany", hacking his way through dense, primeval forests and plodding through bare and wind-swept mountain passes, preaching in tribal camps and villages, baptising converts, demolishing pagan shrines and "chopping down a numinous German tree", as Eleanor S. Duckett so happily puts it, is a far more intelligible and attractive figure than the founder of the territorial German episcopate, or the papal legate presiding over a reforming synod in Gaul, or the stalwart defender of the Roman canons against false teachers, lawless priests and complacent bishops. Nevertheless, these activities were the very things that made durable his work as an apostle and evangelist. Without them his legacy would have been incomplete and his personality imperfectly integrated. It is his consummate genius as a "master-builder" which differentiates him from his Irish and Frankish forerunners, who, either because they lacked the capacity for organisation or despised it as mundane or pedestrian, left no permanent memorial of their often heroic and saintly lives. "Important as his apostolic work was for Germany, his organising and reforming activity was of greater consequence", is the verdict of a twentieth century German authority on the subject, Wilhelm Levison. Like St Augustine of Canterbury Boniface was a great missionary, probably a greater; like Theodore of Tarsus he was a superb administrator and farsighted statesman. He was unique in the fact that he combined in an extraordinary way the rôles of Augustine and Theodore in one.

Boniface was probably over sixty years old when the pope commissioned him to work in Bavaria, and it is noteworthy that Willibald describes him as "enfeebled by old age" on the return journey from Rome. Yet his greatest and most constructive work remained to be done. After spending eight or nine months in Rome, he left it in February 739, "laden with gifts and relics". More precious than these, he took back with him a large number of recruits for the German mission field, Anglo-Saxons, Franks and Bavarians. The next fifteen years of his life were packed full of intense and laborious activity. He had already once visited Bavaria in 735 in his capacity as regionary archbishop and had gained the approval of its Frankish duke, Hucbert (or Hugobert), and a promise of help for his work. The clearer definition of his authority contained in the papal mandate of 738 would greatly facilitate his labours. He could now count on the support both of the local Frankish governors and of the Roman See. For in Bavaria he was faced with problems essentially different from those he had solved in Hesse and Thuringia.

Christianity had been introduced into the country in the early part of the seventh century in the wake of the Frankish conquest and settlement. The gospel had been spread in

D

almost all parts of the region through the itinerant preaching of the Frankish monks, St Rupert of Worms, St Emmeram and St Corbinian. Their diverse activities were
wholly independent and unco-ordinated, in the good old
Irish tradition, but as a result churches and centres of
Christian teaching were set up in Regensburg (Ratisbon),
Salzburg (which was then included in the Bavarian duchy),
Freising and other places. Bishops were consecrated or
brought in from outside, but these again, in accordance
with Celtic practice, were either attached to monasteries or
roamed about the countryside as free-lance preachers. No
attempt was made to establish dioceses with fixed boundaries and regular organisation, and contacts with Rome
were infrequent and uncertain. Nor was the political situation in the duchy favourable to orderly religious progress.

Frankish troops patrolled the country and Frankish
garrisons were installed in the fortified towns. Odilo, who
succeeded to the dukedom in 736, was constantly on the
watch for an opportunity of throwing off the yoke of Charles
Martel. Such were the difficult and unstable conditions in
which Boniface arrived to take up his work in 739. Odilo
was prepared to be a friend and patron of ecclesiastical reform, but only on his own terms; so long as it did not conflict with his determination to be master in his own duchy.
He was all in favour of the establishment of a provincial
church in Bavaria after the Roman model, if it would in
any way strengthen his claim to political independence of
the Frankish crown. He conceived that it might, provided
he played his cards well. Events proved him wrong, but in
the early years of their association he and Boniface found it
possible, within limits, to work together. But Boniface held
the trump card, not Odilo. The military might of Charles
Martel was the factor of supreme importance, and for purely
secular interests this would undoubtedly be thrown on the
side of Rome and the local champion of Rome's cause, Archbishop Boniface himself. It was the first time that Boniface

had been caught in the conflicting currents of secular politics, and the experience gained played no small part in widening his political horizon and developing his capacity as a statesman.

The archbishop lost no time in getting to grips with the confused situation. There were bishops without sees, and sees without bishops. Soon after his arrival Boniface consecrated three new bishops with fixed sees and divided the whole country into four territorial dioceses. In so doing he fitted the ecclesiastical framework on to existing political units. The sites of the new sees were old Roman townships or fortified camps, with monasteries adjacent or within easy reach. The three new bishops seem to have been previously connected with local Christian communities. Gaibald was nominated bishop of Regensburg; John, bishop of Salzburg, and Erembert, brother of Corbinian, was appointed to Freising. Vivilo, bishop of Passau, who had been previously consecrated in Rome by Gregory III, was confirmed in possession of his see. These appointments and dispositions were made in 739. A fourth bishopric was set up two years later at Eichstätt, in which Boniface installed his cousin, Willibald, as regionary bishop for the Bavarian Nordgau, a backward and still half pagan area. After strange and romantic adventures in Palestine and the East Willibald had become a monk at Monte Cassino in 729. When Boniface visited Rome in 738, he persuaded Willibald to quit the monastery and join him in Germany. But the appointment of a few territorial bishops did not in itself mean that the Bavarian Church had been firmly founded. Boniface had also to provide a centralised system of administration and institutions in which a corporate church life could be expressed or realised. Machinery for summoning provincial synods was non-existent for the simple reason that the church had hitherto lacked an archbishop of metropolitan status. Boniface was still a regionary archbishop with no fixed seat, but he had been granted metropolitan

authority and, over and above this, full legatine powers for
all Germany east of the Rhine. He could thus summon in
the pope's name a plenary council of the Bavarian Church.
There is no doubt that he did so, for Gregory III mentions
such a council as imminent in his letter of 29th October
739 (*Ep.* 45) and invests Boniface with full Apostolic
authority for the occasion. But the place and date of the
council are unknown, and its canons have not come down
to us. It was probably held in 740, and appears to have been
the only council held in all the wide dominions of the
Frankish realm during Charles Martel's long rule! We can
get some idea of the kind of problem the council dealt with
from hints in the papal letter referred to above. After ex-
pressing whole-hearted approval of the measures taken by
Boniface to organise a territorial episcopate, Gregory
touches on the problem of irregular or uncertain ordina-
tions. Character and suitability for office, he suggests,
should be the main test, the implication being that, in the
abnormal conditions prevailing in Bavaria, Boniface ought
not to interpret the Roman canons too strictly where purely
formal or technical impediments were found to exist. It was
sage counsel, clearly and cogently expressed, and the pope
goes on to quicken the archbishop's missionary zeal. "You
are not at liberty, brother, to tarry in one place when your
work there is finished," but, "wherever God shall open to
you a road to the salvation of souls, carry on with your
preaching." It was somewhat gratuitous advice to offer a
man of Boniface's stamp, but evidently Gregory was anxious
lest he should become immersed in the technical details of
administration at too early a stage, when there were still
lapsed or lukewarm Christians to be reclaimed and pockets
of heathenism where the gospel must be preached. Fortunately there was no danger of Boniface forgetting this.

Concurrently with the organisation of the diocesan
episcopate and the construction of a centralised system of
administration went the plantation of the monastic life.

This, above all else, was what Bavaria sorely needed, centres of corporate prayer and worship, where the piety and asceticism instilled into their converts by the wandering Frankish preachers of the past could become stabilised and integrated into the tradition of the Catholic Church. This, as we have seen, was work dear to the heart of Boniface, and much of his time in these crowded and difficult years was devoted to it. Up and down the country, wherever suitable sites could be found and the land purchased or presented, houses of religion for men and women were erected, and schools and seminaries attached for the training of priests, lay teachers and women workers. The work continued to make good progress after Boniface's death, and it is calculated that nearly a hundred monasteries were established in Bavaria between 740 and 778. The pattern of monastic development was the same as Boniface had traced out earlier, and was to perfect later, in Hesse and Thuringia. Always the ordering of the religious life went hand in hand with the formation of religious communities, and the closest of links was forged between bishopric and monastery in the practical tasks of pastoral ministration. All this laborious, but constructive, work was accomplished within two short years. By 741 the foundations were well and truly laid. The church in Bavaria never looked back, despite political vicissitudes and the inroads made from time to time by heresy and false teaching. In Crawford's words, it was now "Catholic in discipline and organisation . . . and the authority of the papal see had become a reality throughout Germany east of the Rhine." Boniface and his mission still had to rely for protection and safety on the sword of Charles Martel, but the church he had established and organised was dependent, not on the Frankish hierarchy, but on Rome.

From these remarkable achievements in Bavaria Boniface turned in 741 to Hesse and Thuringia, bent on accomplishing a similar task among his own converts. There too the local churches were in need of discipline and organisation and the country lacked territorial dioceses and sufficient centres of monastic life. That same year he created three new sees with the approval of the pope and the gracious permission of Charles Martel. He had some difficulty in finding suitable sites, for the country had few towns of any size and the pope had forbidden him to erect bishoprics in thinly populated areas or where the numbers of Christians were small (*Ep.* 28). He chose Buraburg, a fortified hill-camp garrisoned by Frankish troops and not far from the monastery of Fritzlar, as the seat of a bishopric for Hesse; Erfurt, conveniently near another monastery, Ohrdruf, for Thuringia proper lying north of the great forest, and Wurzburg, a rising town on the Main, for southern Thuringia. For two of these new sees he consecrated Anglo-Saxons as bishops. Witta, one of his earliest disciples, was set over Buraburg, while Burchard of Malmesbury was installed at Wurzburg. The name of the first bishop of Erfurt is unknown. The diocesan framework of the provincial church of Hesse-Thuringia was thus all but complete by 742. In this church of his own creation and in the Bavarian Church, which he had reformed and organised, he now had eight suffragans, while a few of the older established bishops in Allemannia also acknowledged his authority. There remained, however, the anomaly that he himself was a metropolitan archbishop without a "metropolis" or archiepiscopal see, and it was long before this defect in his status was rectified. During these years Boniface was equally busy fostering the growth and expansion of the monastic life. Amöneburg, Fritzlar and Ohrdruf by this time harboured well-ordered and flourishing communities, and there were some struggling, smaller houses. But the influx of monks and nuns from England and the Frankish realm made it necessary to "colonise" and to create for them new and independent foundations in the remoter areas where their services as missionaries were most required, Eichstätt, Willibald's episcopal seat, was an early example of such a house, and some years later Heidenheim, a double monastery, constructed on the Anglo-Saxon model, became an important centre under the rule of Willibald's brother, Winnebald, whom Boniface had persuaded to leave England and join him in Germany, where he was reunited with his far-travelled brother. He had been carefully trained by Boniface in "parochial" and pastoral work before being placed in charge of this double community. On his death in 761 his sister, Walpurgis, took over the reins of government.

Heidenheim was a large and prosperous house, but it pales into insignificance beside the abbey of Fulda, which is inseparably linked with the name and fame of Boniface. It enshrines his mortal remains and in a deeper sense than this it is his supreme memorial. It was the child of his travail, and yet the scene of his happiest moments and his deepest spiritual experience. In the later stages of the campaign it was the G.H.Q. of the German mission field. It was designed to serve as a model for every Benedictine house in Germany, to be, in fact, the German Monte Cassino. It was even more than this, for it became ultimately the chief centre of Anglo-Saxon religious culture on the Continent, and as such it is the supreme manifestation of Boniface's conviction that the monastic life and institutions were indispensable for the building up of a Christian civilisation in Germany. Fulda must therefore loom large in any assessment of Boniface as an ecclesiastical organiser and statesman.

The story of Fulda really begins with the coming of Sturm, a Bavarian lad of noble birth committed by his parents to the care of Boniface during the archbishop's first sojourn in the land in 735. Boniface placed him in the monastery of Fritzlar to be educated under Abbot Wigbert. He is mentioned in one of the saint's letters (*Ep.* 40) written in 737 or 738 to arrange the affairs of Fritzlar after Wigbert's death: "Let Sturm take charge of the kitchen". In due course he was ordained priest and worked for three years in

the Hessian mission. But the desire to embrace the monastic
life worked strongly in him. He yearned for a retreat far
from the haunts of men. Boniface, who had for some time
been planning to build a great abbey to serve as a focal
point for missionary work in the south-east corner of
Thuringia and to link up with the numerous houses already
established in Bavaria, saw in Sturm the very man for the
task. He encouraged him in his vocation and sent him out
with two companions into the wild and unexplored country
south of Fritzlar to look for a suitable site for building. The
first two expeditions were abortive. After much toilsome
wandering and many adventures Sturm and his companions
found what seemed to them an admirable site, but Boniface
rejected it as being exposed to the ravages of Saxon marau-
ders. Sturm then set out a third time on a lone trek yet
deeper into the virgin forest till at last his experienced eye
lighted on the ideal spot, a broad valley hemmed in by the
mountains from which flowed into it the torrential waters of
the River Fulda. The soil was fertile and the scenery of un-
wonted grandeur and beauty. Boniface came to view the
site, approved Sturm's choice and successfully petitioned
Carloman, the Frankish duke of Austrasia, for the free
conveyance of the land. In January 744 he came again with
an army of workmen to clear the forest and prepare the
ground. In April of the same year building operations
began. Bit by bit a stone church, dedicated to the Holy
Saviour, and the monastic buildings began to take shape,
and a small band of monks arrived to take possession. The
archbishop would come and inspect progress whenever he
could spare the time, and instruct the monks in the Rule of
St Benedict. In 748 he dispatched Sturm to Italy to study
the Benedictine life at first hand in Rome and Monte
Cassino. On his return two years later Sturm was duly appointed abbot of Fulda. The growth of the abbey was
phenomenal. When Sturm died in 779, it housed upwards
of four hundred monks. The venture was an unqualified

success and reflects equal credit on Sturm and his master.
Boniface took legitimate pride in these monks of his who
strove to live the Benedictine life in all its pristine purity. He
grew to love the place and spent much time in retreat there
in his later years, living and working with the brethren in
house and field and farm, joining them in choir for the daily
offices and taking solitary walks in the neighbourhood.
Especially did he frequent a certain hill overlooking the
abbey in the valley beneath. Here he had built a hut or
cell, wherein he could read and meditate upon Holy Writ
without fear of interruption, or commune with God in
prayer and so draw fresh hope and courage for the tasks that
lay ahead. To Pope Zacharias he wrote in 751 (*Ep.* 86),
"There is a wooded placed situated in a vast wilderness and
in the midst of the people to whom we are preaching. There
we have settled a band of monks living under the Rule of
St Benedict who are building a monastery. They abstain
altogether from meat and wine and spirits. They have no
servants, but are content with the labours of their own
hands . . . Here I propose, with your gracious permission,
to rest my weary, age-worn limbs for a little time, and after
my death to be buried here." He was determined to protect
the abbey, so far as he could, from the danger of ruin or
degradation overtaking it after his death, so he besought
the pope to grant it a privilege of immunity. The request
was probably made in the latter part, now unfortunately
missing, of the letter quoted above. Pope Zacharias assented
to his petition and issued that same year a papal charter
(*Ep.* 89) granting the abbey of Fulda exemption from episcopal authority and placing it unreservedly and irrevocably
under the direct and plenary jurisdiction of the Holy See.
Boniface has been severely criticised for this action. It is
true that some Frankish abbeys had before this received
privileges of immunity from episcopal jurisdiction, but none,
up till now, had been placed under direct obedience to
Rome, and this was an unprecedented innovation.

Nevertheless, the action fits in with Boniface's general policy of maintaining the closest possible links between the infant German churches and the authority of the pope. It should be judged in the light of its success in promoting ecclesiastical stability and autonomy in an age when the secular power was continually encroaching on religious freedom. In this connection it is significant that the papal privilege was never endorsed by the Frankish crown, the existing charter of Pippin the Short purporting to confirm it being a forgery of half a century later.

The deaths of Charles Martel and Gregory III within a month of each other in the autumn of 741 had a marked effect both on the position of Boniface and the fortunes of the German mission. That of Charles Martel removed a notable figure from the stage of history. He died at the height of his power and prestige in the Romano-barbarian world. He had been more than king among the Franks, although he had never worn the crown. He had been a bulwark in the defence of Christendom against the forces of Islam on the west and of heathen barbarism in the east, where he had considerably extended the Frankish frontier. Boniface himself had always recognised how greatly his labours in Germany depended for success on the maintenance of peace and order which only Charles and his Frankish garrisons could ensure. He expressed himself in this sense in a letter to Daniel, bishop of Winchester (*Ep.* 63), written probably within a year of Charles' death. "Without the protection of the prince of the Franks," he wrote, "I can neither rule the people of the Church nor defend the priests and clerks, monks and nuns; nor can I prevent the practice of pagan rites and the sacrilegious worship of idols without his mandate and the awe inspired by his name." The words in themselves do not prove much. As has often been pointed out, they are susceptible of a double interpretation. Boniface may have been recording his appreciation of the services Charles had rendered. On the other hand he may have been voicing the opinion that Charles might have given help of a more positive kind to the German mission instead of confining it to the military sphere. Certainly in his later years Charles' enthusiasm for the cause, if he ever had any, cooled considerably, and one is left with the impression that he might have done more for Boniface than he actually did. His attitude of reserve and detachment contrasts unfavourably with the cordial relations which had existed between his father, Pippin of Heristal and Willibrord, and still more markedly with the wholehearted support accorded to Boniface by his sons, Carloman and Pippin the Short.

The long-term effects of Charles' death were thus by no means detrimental to the German mission, although for the moment it brought a recrudescence of political strife and anarchy in the Bavarian duchy, which seemed likely to threaten the security of the provincial church. For Duke Odilo and the malcontent Frankish magnates of Bavaria and Franconia rebelled against Carloman and Pippin. Odilo even made overtures to the new pope, Zacharias, who for a while toyed with the idea that the duke might become his ally in the struggle with the Lombards in Italy, against whom Charles Martel had recently refused to take up arms at the pope's behest. Zacharias was imprudent enough to make a friendly gesture to the rebel duke by despatching a papal legate to Bavaria and consecrating a new bishop without reference to Boniface. In this dangerous and invidious situation Boniface maintained a proper and statesmanlike neutrality. He refused to be drawn into the political arena. A single false move might have imperilled the future of the Bavarian Church and perhaps of the German mission as a whole. While the political situation remained confused and unstable, the spiritual gains of the past few years could not be consolidated and no further progress could be made in the missionary campaign. The situation was clarified by Pippin's decisive victory over the rebels, and Odilo was only restored to his duchy after sacrificing a good deal of territory and accepting terms of strict feudal dependence on the Frankish crown. Henceforth he abandoned his particularist policy in ecclesiastical affairs, and Boniface's authority over the Bavarian Church once more accorded with his status as a Frankish archbishop. The issue of events was a complete vindication of the shrewd and cautious statesmanship of Boniface and a condemnation of the impolitic and adventurous action of Zacharias. It is easy to see why a certain coolness between the archbishop and Rome marks the opening years of the new pontificate.

Zacharias was certainly a pope of some consequence. Greek by descent, though Italian by birth, he is described as "learned and eloquent", but he was primarily a politician and a diplomat by training and temperament. The closer and friendlier relations between the Frankish state and the Holy See, which developed in his pontificate, certainly owed something to him, even if greater credit should be given to Boniface. It is significant, however, that Hauck judges Zacharias to have been "a smaller man than Gregory III". His German policy followed the broad lines of his predecessors, and he gave steady support to Archbishop Boniface and his suffragans. Yet there was never quite the confidence and intimacy between Boniface and Zacharias which had existed between the archbishop and previous popes. It is possible to detect in Boniface's correspondence with Zacharias a note of criticism which throws into sharp relief the filial obedience which normally governed the archbishop's dealings with the Apostolic See and is displayed in the letters exchanged between him and the two Gregorys. Early in 742 Boniface wrote to congratulate Zacharias on his accession to the papal chair (*Ep.* 50). "It is our earnest desire," he assures the pope, "to maintain the Catholic Faith and the unity of the Roman Church." He asks for papal confirmation of the three bishops recently appointed in Hesse and Thuringia, informs the pope of Carloman's intention to hold a reforming council of the church in Austrasia, and requests the pope's advice and permission for him to proceed in the matter. He paints a lurid picture of the abuses and corruptions rife in the Frankish Church, where no council had met during the preceding eighty years and metropolitan authority was virtually suspended. He asks for a formal mandate from the pope authorising him, in his capacity as legate of the Apostolic See, to judge and sentence clerks convicted of evil life and worldly activities unbecoming to men of religion, like engaging in war and hunting. He then asserts, with surprising lack of tact and without a word of apology, that it is commonly reported in Germany that the Roman Church is not wholly free from evil practices of a pagan and superstitious character. Such things are a scandal and an offence to the German Christians and a serious hindrance to the preaching of the gospel in the mission field. Will the pope provide him with an effective answer to these charges? The letter ends with some Latin verses of the archbishop's own composition presumably intended to soothe the pope's injured feelings. Possibly piqued by the lofty and independent tone adopted by the archbishop, but more likely preoccupied with the eternal problem of Lombard aggression in Italy, Zacharias delayed answering the letter for nearly fifteen months. His reply (*Ep.* 51) is dated 1st April 743. It is a somewhat lengthy screed, the chief points of which may be summarised as follows. First, the pope expresses doubts as to the wisdom of erecting three new sees in Hesse and Thuringia, in view of the sparseness of the population and the comparative insignificance of the sites selected. It is as though the pope were bent on showing that Boniface himself was not immune from criticism. Nevertheless, he could do no other than ratify the appointments already made. Secondly, he approves the project for a reforming council in Austrasia and duly authorises Boniface as his legate to suspend and punish clerks convicted of worldliness, corruption

and immorality. (The council had by this time been held
and Boniface had acted on his own initiative.) Finally the
pope indignantly denies the charge that heathen superstitions and idolatrous practices abound in Rome. They
were effectively dealt with by his predecessor, Gregory III,
and he, Zacharias, is keeping strict watch against a possible
recrudescence of the evil. The whole affair may perhaps be
regarded as "a storm in a teacup", but Boniface was not the
man to utter criticism lightly against the Roman Church
which he reverenced and admired, and to which he and the
German mission owed so much. The episode is interesting
as evidence that Boniface retained an open mind in his dealings with Rome, and the charge of servility and obsequious-
ness, which has sometimes been brought against him, is not
substantiated by the facts. He yielded to none of his contemporaries in faith, loyalty and obedience towards the
Apostolic See, but his was the free and voluntary submission
of "a missionary statesman in the service of Rome".

The accession of Carloman and Pippin to joint power in
the Frankish realm in 741 vastly improved and strengthened
the relations between Boniface and the secular government.
Governing in the name of Childeric III, the Merovingian
puppet king, the two brothers divided their power territorially. Carloman, the elder, ruled Austrasia and the Ger-
manic lands to the east of the Rhine, while Pippin held the
reins of authority in Neustria, Burgundy, Provence and
Aquitaine. Both brothers were able men and worked well
together, though they differed somewhat in character.
Pippin was a warrior, like his father, Charles Martel, but he
possessed, as events were to show, an even greater aptitude
for politics. Carloman's disposition and abilities were more
suited to the ecclesiastical sphere. He was a sincere and dis-
interested patron and defender of Holy Church and a

generous benefactor to churches and abbeys. It was fortunate for Boniface that the eastern half of the Frankish
realm fell to Carloman, for it meant that, as head of the
German mission, he had to deal with a ruler of spiritual
insight, who clearly discerned the intrinsic importance of
the work in which he was engaged. Carloman gave him
moral as well as material support. Moreover, this son of
Charles Martel was a zealot for church reform and was
determined to undertake through the agency of Boniface a
drastic and far-reaching reformation of the Frankish Church
in his dominions. None was better fitted than Boniface, by
character, experience and status, to tackle this formidable
task. It was through his personal intimacy with Carloman
that he became the dominant influence in the Austrasian
Church, and that influence was before long extended to
Neustria where Pippin held sway.

The period of "Home Missions" in Boniface's career, as
it may be called, opened with the first Austrasian council
summoned by Carloman and held probably in April 742.
For the next seven years Gaul was the chief scene of Boniface's activities. He did not, of course, neglect the needs of
Germany, but he left the direction of the mission field more
and more to the bishops he had set up there. The work
which he was doing in Gaul under the patronage of Carloman and Pippin was, for the moment, of greater, even of
crucial importance. The long-term effect of his reforms in
the Frankish Church was to strengthen the links binding the
Franks to the Papacy in the sphere of politics no less than
in that of religion. His work as an ecclesiastical reformer is
thus a component part of his legacy as a statesman. Boniface was under no illusions as to the magnitude of the task
he had undertaken. It was comparatively easy to issue reforming canons; it was much more difficult to get them
properly carried out in face of the stubborn opposition of
powerful prelates like the bishops of Mainz and Trier and
the culpable indifference of most of the other Frankish

bishops, many of whom disdained to attend the early
synods. It was just here that the strong and consistent support of the Frankish princes was invaluable. It was Carloman who convoked the Austrasian councils of 742 and 743.
He was present at both, and published their decisions in the
form of state capitularies. Both these assemblies were
"mixed councils", that is to say, the lay magnates of the
land participated in them together with the clergy. Boniface
presided over them in his dual capacity of Frankish archbishop and papal legate, and his metropolitan authority
over all east Frankish sees was thus acknowledged. If the
decrees issued by the synods remained in some cases a dead
letter, at least they served as a manifesto of the reforming
programme sponsored by the Austrasian government, and
in time acquired the force of precedents. Moreover, Carloman's example was copied by Pippin in his own dominions.
Eager to show himself as keen on ecclesiastical reform as his
brother, Pippin summoned in March 742 the council of
Soissons. There is nothing in the documents to show that
Boniface attended this Neustrian synod. But even if he was
not present in person, his spirit inspired and directed its
deliberations. Like its Austrasian prototypes this was also a
"mixed council", and the lay magnates present attested its
decrees. The most important act of this council was its provision for the establishment of three metropolitan arch-
bishoprics at Rouen, Rheims and Sens. Pope Zacharias gave
his assent to the proposal (*Ep.* 57), but the scheme was never
carried out. For some unexplained reason Pippin changed
his mind, and Boniface was placed in the humiliating position of having to write to the pope a second time requesting
him to modify the plan by restricting the use of the pallium
to Grimo of Rouen alone. Zacharias, who probably felt that
he had been made to look rather foolish, expressed his as-
tonishment and irritation at Pippin's *volte-face* with some
vigour (*Ep.* 58).

The council of Soissons was followed next year by another

of unknown location. This too was a "mixed council", with the difference that on this occasion prelates and lay magnates from both Neustria and Austrasia attended in force. It may therefore be regarded as a council of the whole Frankish Church. Boniface certainly presided over it, but the information available concerning it is scanty, since its canons or capitularies are no longer extant. The disciplinary decrees of earlier councils were confirmed, but the chief topics of debate seem to have been doctrinal and administrative. The council condemned as heretical the teachings of two eccentric and fanatical wandering preachers named Aldebert and Clement, who both claimed to have received episcopal orders. Their tenets apparently had little in common and they seem to have acted independently, Aldebert in Neustria and Clement in Austrasia. They both figure prominently in Boniface's correspondence with the pope in these years. They seduced so many Christians from the Catholic Faith and in general caused Boniface so much trouble that he was constrained to report their cases to Rome through his trusty envoy, Denehard. A Roman synod held later that year confirmed the sentence of deprivation of episcopal orders and imprisonment in the cloister passed in Gaul against the two "heresiarchs", but they escaped from custody and resumed their preaching unmolested. Pope Zacharias wrote to Pippin in 747 (*Ep.* 77) ordering them to be sent to Rome for further examination, if they continued contumacious. After this they apparently ceased their preaching activities, for nothing more is heard of them. It is an interesting example of the continual struggle Boniface had to wage against superstition and false doctrine, but a deeper investigation of the subject would hardly be appropriate here. The Frankish council of 745 was also concerned with a plan to establish an effective metropolitan centre for Germany. The see of Cologne was vacant, and it was proposed to install Boniface therein and make it an archbishopric. Although approved and ratified

E

by the pope (*Ep.* 60), the proposal aroused such strong opposition from Boniface's enemies among the Frankish bishops, many of whom were influential at court, that it had to be dropped. Instead Boniface was a little later recompensed with the see of Mainz. It was not however, until 780, long after his death, that Mainz was raised to the dignity of an archbishopric. For the remainder of his life Boniface was still a regionary archbishop functioning by virtue of his legatine authority.

The last of the reforming synods held in Gaul during the lifetime of Boniface was the general council of 747. It took place early in the year, before Carloman's sudden retirement from public life to become a monk in Italy made Pippin sole ruler of the Franks. It was a fuller and more representative body than any of its predecessors. All the Frankish bishops were present, friends and foes of Boniface alike, and the archbishop was well supported by his suffragans and clergy from the German mission. It is doubtful, however, whether any lay magnates attended. Again we have to lament the absence of conciliar decrees. The agenda has to be reconstructed from information gleaned from the Frankish correspondence of the pope and from a letter written by Boniface to Cuthbert, archbishop of Canterbury, (*Ep.* 78) which summarises the council's decisions. No new reforms of any importance seem to have issued from the debates; the council is rather a summation of the results already achieved. Boniface and his opponents seem to have become reconciled with each other, and "a charter of true and orthodox profession and of Catholic unity" was drawn up, subscribed by all present and sent to the pope. It includes a promise of full and unlimited obedience to the Apostolic See and the Roman canons. This document may be regarded as setting the seal on Boniface's work in this field. The prevalent confusion and anarchy in the Frankish Church were ended. Particular interests and obligations had been forced to give place to the needs of the Church as a whole. The ground-plan of reform had been accepted and endorsed by the Frankish hierarchy in its corporate capacity. Order and obedience under papal authority were henceforth to be enforced on all ranks of the clergy. The reformation of church life, doctrine and administration had been vindicated in principle, and machinery constructed for orderly religious progress. The specific reforms enacted in the various councils had yet to be put into operation effectively, since they depended on the gradual purification of ecclesiastical personnel, from bishops and abbots down to parish priests and monks, and this process naturally took time. It was still necessary after 747 for Pope Zacharias to write to the Frankish bishops (*Ep*. 82) admonishing them on their duty of filial obedience to their archbishop, and to the lay magnates (*Ep*. 83) exhorting them to give him all possible aid in the cause of reform.

The difficulties which Boniface continued to encounter in the discharge of his functions as metropolitan archbishop and papal legate during these years should not be overlooked. They were very real, whether they sprang from the factious opposition of recalcitrant bishops and corrupt clerics, or from the dissemination of error and false teaching, as in the case of Aldebert and Clement, who were protected by powerful interests in the Frankish court, or as in the case of Virgil of Salzburg, who was vindicated by Pope Zacharias from the charge of heresy brought against him by Boniface, promoted bishop of that city in 755 and canonised after his death. From such examples it may be inferred that the archbishop's authority over the Frankish and German Churches was by no means so great or so secure as he could have wished, or has sometimes been assumed. In some matters he encountered opposition from the Frankish rulers, in others even from the pope. Yet nothing could efface the permanent value of the work he had accomplished through the Frankish councils and through his personal intimacy with, and ascendancy over, Carloman and Pippin. He had accustomed them to the idea of referring questions of church order to Rome for consideration. Envoys went backwards and forwards with increasing frequency as the years progressed. The pope gave counsel and exhortation, now to the secular rulers and magnates, now to the bishops. A bond of common interest was established between the Frankish government and the Apostolic See which would have been impossible in the days of Charles Martel, and it was becoming more and more recognised by the Frankish episcopate that only through co-operation with Rome and in communion with her could the Frankish Church prosper.

This change in the relations between church and state in the Frankish realm brought new difficulties, both personal and political, in its train. Boniface was compelled in the execution of his duties to pay occasional visits to the Frankish court, and often he was sorely troubled in conscience at having to meet there and to mix with worldly and corrupt ecclesiastics whose fellowship he had foresworn in the oath taken to Gregory II at the time of his consecration as bishop. He gave utterance to his scruples on this point in a letter (*Ep.* 86) to Pope Zacharias written in 751. "This promise I have in part maintained, but I have not been able wholly to fulfil it. In spirit I have kept my oath, since I have not agreed with them nor taken part in their counsels. But in the letter I have been unable to avoid contact with them altogether, because when I have had to visit the Frankish court on urgent ecclesiastical business, I have found there men with whom I would rather not have consorted. Nevertheless, I have never partaken with them in the Holy Communion of the Body and Blood of Christ." These journeys to court tended to involve him, much against his will, in affairs of state. It was natural that he should be consulted by the secular rulers, but he neither aspired to, nor acquired political influence under Pippin the Short, although historians have sometimes credited him with it. There is no evidence that he played any part in the negotiations with the pope which prepared the way for the dynastic revolution of 751 wherein Childeric III, the last of the Merovingians, was deposed and Pippin at long last mounted the throne of the Franks. Pippin's envoys to Rome for that purpose were Fulrad, abbot of St Denis and Burchard, bishop of Wurzburg. It is true that the latter was one of Boniface's most trusted disciples and experienced agents, but the fact that he had often been despatched to Rome by Boniface on the business of the German Church, and was thus personally known to Pope Zacharias, sufficiently explains Pippin's choice of him for this delicate diplomatic mission. Doubts have even been expressed as to the truth of the statement in the Frankish annals that it was Boniface who actually crowned Pippin king, but the best modern authorities unite in giving an affirmative answer to this question. Even so, this proves no more than that Boniface, with his immense personal prestige and his dual status of Frankish archbishop and papal legate, was regarded as the fit and proper person to perform the ceremony. In crowning Pippin he represented both the pope and the Frankish people, and the act was the consummation of his ecclesiastical policy. Ever since his first visit to Charles Martel in the early days of the German mission he had consistently striven to promote understanding and friendship between the Franks and the Roman See. His success in reforming and reorganising the Frankish Church was the means whereby this re-orientation in the politics of Western Christendom was achieved. The alliance between the Frankish crown and the Papacy owes more to Boniface than to either of the two contracting parties, king or pope. It was the foundation on which Charlemagne was to build his theocratic empire in A.D. 800 fifty years later. This is the measure of Boniface's greatness as an ecclesiastical statesman.

III. BONIFACE: THE MAN AND THE SAINT

The reader of a modern biography, accustomed to being provided with a wealth of detail concerning the life and personality of his hero, and unfamiliar with the more limited aims and wholly different technique of the medieval author, is apt to come away from the perusal of a Latin *Life* of some medieval worthy with feelings of impatience, bewilderment and frustration. So often the writer fails to tell us the things we want to know or to answer the questions that spring naturally to mind. At best we are left with an idealised portrait of the real man, and we are indeed fortunate if the image be not distorted by eulogy or flattery, or blurred by an indiscriminate and uncritical use of anecdote and fable. Too often, and too easily, medieval biography degenerates into mere hagiography: the *Life* becomes a *Legend*. Willibald's *Life of St Boniface*—the only contemporary, or near contemporary, account of the saint—is no exception. As one would expect, the author concentrates on the mental and moral progress of his hero and the characteristic features of his spiritual life. As a churchman Willibald shared the predilections and prejudices of his age and caste. He was more interested in the graces of the soul than in the lineaments of the body. In consequence he tells us nothing about Boniface's personal appearance, habits and conversation, whether he was tall or short, stout or slender, dark or fair; and in the eighth century distinguished men were not painted in oils or carved in stone or marble. We can, of course, deduce from the story of his active and adventurous life that he was endowed with physical strength and stamina well above the average, but we are nowhere specifically told so. On the contrary, Willibald's few references to the saint's constitution suggest that for many years before his death he experienced in full measure the physical suffering natural to advancing age, and that the herculean labours of his later years were only made possible by a veritable triumph of mind over body—a conclusion naturally congenial to an ecclesiastical biographer, and perhaps not altogether devoid of truth. The lack of colour and precision in Willibald's description of Boniface's personality may in part be due to the fact that he was not personally acquainted with his hero; yet, as he himself tells us in the first chapter of his book, he took the trouble, in gathering his materials, to meet and talk with many of the saint's closest friends and disciples, and others who had known him well. Nevertheless, the fact remains that it would be quite impossible for a modern writer to recreate the personality and character of Boniface, if he had to depend solely, or even mainly, on this contemporary *Life*. Fortunately a second and far richer source is open to him in the saint's correspondence.

The *Letters* have been described by Sir Frank Stenton as "the most remarkable body of correspondence which has survived from the Dark Ages". Over a hundred letters are printed in Tangl's edition of the original Latin, and many others, as we can tell, have perished in the course of the centuries. A good proportion of those extant consist of letters written to, and by, the popes, and their importance for the history of the German mission and the politics of the Frankish kingdom has already been shown. But these precious literary relics of the age have a wider and deeper significance. They prove that Boniface had a large circle of friends and acquaintances and maintained a lively and intelligent interest in the affairs of his native land no less than in those which were his immediate concern in Gaul and Germany. The letters were written to, and received from, an astonishing variety of correspondents, drawn from all ranks and classes of society, and ranging from popes and kings at the top to humble monks and nuns at the bottom. In his answers Boniface treats them all with the respect and consideration due to their station with filial piety, fraternal fellowship or paternal solicitude. The letters afford abundant evidence of his strongly marked personality, of his unusual capacity for love and friendship, and of the affection, good will and enthusiasm which he could evoke in others. They display too his consummate gifts of leadership and direction, his exalted sense of duty, his wisdom, tolerance and generosity, his breadth of view and command of detail. But they also show that he depended on others, to a far greater extent than we might have expected, for material aid and spiritual succour, for books and food and raiment, no less than for prayer and intercession and that mysterious kinship of the soul that binds together men and women of highly developed spiritual insight in a kind of earthly anticipation of the communion of saints. Not that Boniface was a great letter-writer, in the sense of a creative literary artist, using the epistolary medium to expound a philosophy of life or to convey his ideas and opinions to a larger audience than a particular correspondent. He was not writing with a view to publication. He was a busy man of action who only used the pen when there was need for him to do so; when he had some urgent problem to deal with, and wanted help and advice, as in many of his earlier letters to the pope or in those addressed to Daniel, bishop of Winchester. Or when there was some "false prophet" to be unmasked and discredited, or some notorious public sinner to be rebuked and summoned to repentance, or some oversensitive conscience to be soothed and quieted. In other words the saint's own letters are for the most part highly practical and objective. The revelation of his personality in them is indirect and unconscious, yet none the less real.

All these features are pre-eminently displayed in the letters he wrote to England. In them *Boniface the man* is most clearly revealed. As one reads these pages, fresh and fragrant still after the lapse of centuries, one can penetrate the secret of his remarkable power and influence over his own kith and kin; one can sense the magnetism which drew men and women by the hundreds from his native Wessex, and not a few from the remoter parts of the Anglo-Saxon realm, to come over and share his life and labours in the German mission field. His contacts with kinsfolk and friends in England remained as close and constant as his busy life as a mission preacher and organiser would permit, and their prayers and presents sustained him in the darkest hours of his conflict with the powers of evil. Through all these letters his sturdy patriotism and abiding love for the homeland, which he was never again to see, shine with a steady and undimmed light. Often he writes in the nostalgic vein of an exile. Always he is jealous for the good name of Englishmen abroad, especially of priests and monks and women who wear the veil. "I rejoice," he wrote in 746 or 747 (*Ep.* 74), "in the good deeds and fame of my nation, but I am aggrieved and afflicted at its sins and shame." In another letter (*Ep.* 78), written shortly afterwards to Cuthbert, archbishop of Canterbury, he deplores the sad scandals which have resulted from the custom of allowing women and nuns to go unescorted on pilgrimage to Rome. Some of them have brought great discredit on the English Church, and it would be well if such pilgrimages were forbidden both by the ecclesiastical authorities and the secular rulers. Generally speaking, however, the letters exchanged with members of the Anglo-Saxon hierarchy have an impersonal character, for they mostly treat of general questions of Church life and order. Yet quite often such letters contain incidental passages of human interest. The letter (*Ep.* 63), written to Daniel of Winchester soon after 742, and already quoted with reference to Charles Martel, is an example of this. Boniface begs the bishop to send him the "Book of the Prophets", which had belonged to his late master, Abbot

Winbert. "You could not," he writes, "give me greater
comfort in my old age or earn for yourself a greater reward.
I cannot obtain in this country a copy of the work suited to
my needs, for with failing eyesight I can no longer read
small and abbreviated script. I ask for this particular volume
because it is written in clear and distinct characters." He
has heard from a Wessex priest lately arrived in Germany
that Daniel himself is grievously afflicted with eye trouble
and has become almost blind: but assuredly God has
stricken him in his bodily eyes only that he may see more
clearly through the windows of the soul. As a token of
affection and remembrance he sends a little gift, "a towel,
not made of pure silk, but mixed with goats' hair, to dry
your feet."

The demand for books is always cropping up in Boniface's
letters to England. In 733 he wrote to Nothelm, archbishop
of Canterbury (*Ep.* 33), asking him to forward a copy of the
Questionnaire sent by St Augustine to Pope Gregory the
Great and of the pope's responses. He has made inquiries at
Rome, but the papal registrars have reported that the
documents are not to be found among Gregory's papers in
the Roman archives. Boniface evidently pursued the subject
further, for we have a letter addressed to him by Cardinal-
deacon Gemmulus from Rome (*Ep.* 54) apologising for the
delay in sending him a copy of Gregory's *Register* and promising to do so forthwith. In 733 Boniface also wrote to
Abbot Dudo (*Ep.* 34), reminding him of their old association as master and pupil and begging the loan of a commentary on St Paul's Epistles. "Though I was but poorly
equipped as a teacher," he writes, "I tried to be the most
devoted of them all, as you yourself are witness. Be mindful
of this devotion and take pity on an old man worn out by a
sea of German troubles. Support me by your prayers, and
aid me by supplying me with the books of Holy Scripture
and the sacred writings of the Fathers. I possess commentaries on only two of St Paul's Epistles, Romans and I

Corinthians. If you have anything else in your monastic library which you think would be useful to me, and of which I am not aware or have no copy, pray let me know . . . and send me any notes of your own." In 746 Boniface was eager to acquire the works of Bede, whose fame was now, nearly fifteen years after his death, widespread in Anglo-Saxon learned circles. Boniface writes to Hwaetbert, Bede's own abbot at Jarrow (*Ep.* 76), begging him for a copy of the commentaries on Holy Scripture and describing the writer as "a lamp of the Church in Biblical studies". A similar request is made in two letters to Egbert, archbishop of York (*Epp.* 75, 91), written within a year of each other. The second of these specifies the particular works he wanted and the purpose for which he needed them —"especially the book of homilies, a convenient and useful manual for us in our preaching, and the Proverbs of Solomon, on which we hear he has written a commentary."

This letter closes with an unexpected and altogether delightful touch, redolent of the saint's humanity and tolerance. Though he abstained from wine and alcoholic liquor on principle and would not permit his monks at Fulda to indulge in them, he now sends Archbishop Egbert by the bearer of his letter "two small casks of wine, in token of mutual affection, beseeching you to use them for a merry day with the brethren." Another remarkable example of his courtesy and solicitude for others is provided in a letter (*Ep.* 101) written by the priest Wigbert to his brother-monks at Glastonbury, enthusiastically describing the welcome he received in Germany. "I wish you to know, dear brethren, that Archbishop Boniface, when he heard of my arrival, came a long way to meet me, and greeted me with the utmost kindness." It was a gracious and generous gesture for a hard worked evangelist to extend to a simple and untried priest, a raw recruit to the mission field, but it is eminently in keeping with Boniface's kindly and considerate disposition, and for all we know it may often have been repeated.

A sterner side of the archbishop's character, his boldness in rebuking vice, even in the highest quarters, is revealed in letters written to that wayward but masterful monarch, Æthelbald of Mercia, the tyrannical overlord of all England betwixt Thames and Humber, whose private life, by common report, was stained with unspeakable vices. There is no hint of this in Boniface's first short letter to him (*Ep.* 69) written in 745 or 746. He begs the king to accept in the spirit of friendship a present of a hawk and two falcons, two shields and two lances. But the letter closes ominously with the words,"Fear God and obey His commandments". A year or eighteen months later Boniface sent him another and longer letter (*Ep.* 73), couched in very different language, chastising the king in withering invective for his evil and dissolute life. True, in the opening paragraphs he praises his defence of the Church, his care for the poor and the oppressed and his liberality in almsgiving, but this is merely the sugar-coating concealing the bitter pill the king had to swallow. The remainder of the letter is a diatribe against his foul crimes and shameless immorality, even against "the holy virgins of God". Unless he truly repents and gives earnest of his purpose to amend his life, he will assuredly perish suddenly and miserably at the hands of Almighty God, like his predecessor, Coelred of Mercia, and like Osred, king of Northumbria, who were plunged without warning into the abyss of hell, there to suffer endless torments. The letter was written in the names of Boniface himself and seven other German bishops of Anglo-Saxon birth, including Burchard of Wurzburg and Willibald of Eichstätt. A covering letter (*Ep.* 74) to a priest named Herefrith, probably one of the Mercian royal chaplains, declares Boniface's motives in sending Æthelbald such a letter to be concern for the good name of the Anglo-Saxon race on the Continent and a genuine desire to promote the king's welfare and that of his people. He returns

to the subject in the letter to Egbert of York already cited
(*Ep.* 75), explaining that he felt compelled to reprove the
erring monarch, not out of pride or arrogance, but because
the pope in his Apostolic commission had ordered him to
rebuke vice in every place and among all peoples and to
strive to bring back sinners to the way of salvation. Two
other crowned heads of the Heptarchy figure among Boniface's correspondents, Ælbwald of East Anglia (*Ep.* 81) and
Æthelbert II of Kent (*Ep.* 105), and this in itself testifies to
the prestige he enjoyed among the secular rulers of England.
King Æthelbert commends himself to the archbishop at
the suggestion of a mutual friend, Abbess Bugga, of whom
more anon. He sends as gifts a silver drinking cup lined with
gold and two woollen cloaks, not, as he naïvely puts it, in
the hope of receiving any gift in return, save the most
salutary one of the saint's prayers. Nevertheless, at the end
of his letter he cannot resist begging the archbishop to pro-
cure for him a pair of falcons, apparently a scarce com-
modity in Kent at that time. Whether or not his expectations were fulfilled, we do not know.

As an example of Boniface's power to awaken enthusiasm
and fervour among his fellow-countrymen for the missionary
campaign in Germany may be cited the inspired letter he
wrote about the year 738, addressed to all the bishops and
clergy of the English Church (*Ep.* 46). Even across the centuries his plaintive eloquence has lost none of its appeal.

"We humbly beseech you," he writes, "to remember
us in your prayers, that we may escape the cunning snares
of the devil and the assaults of wicked men, that the word
of God may go forward and be glorified. We beg you to
be instant in prayer that God and our Lord Jesus Christ,
*Who willeth that all men should be saved and come to the
knowledge of the truth,* may turn the hearts of the heathen
Saxons to the Catholic Faith . . . and gather them
among the children of Mother Church. Take pity on
them, for they themselves are now saying, 'We are of one

blood and of one bone with you' . . . Be it known to you, moreover, that in making this appeal I have the approval, assent and blessing of two pontiffs of the Apostolic See.''

It was "a cry from the heart", and it was answered in a most practical and effective way, for it was this letter that caused the remarkable exodus of priests, monks and nuns from England to the Continent which led to the establishment of an Anglo-Saxon "religious colony" in Germany.

Some of the nuns and women workers who answered this call had already corresponded with Boniface in earlier years, and the letters in this group are among the most charming and intimate in the whole collection. They manifest the saint in gentler mood and illustrate the striking appeal which his personality made to women. By this means in later years he was able to make use of their services to an unprecedented extent in the all-important work of religious education overseas. Even those of them who stayed at home seem to have been chiefly occupied in training recruits for the German mission field, a task which they discharged with conscientious zeal and conspicuous success. Foremost among these are the two abbesses, Eadburg and Bugga. It does not seem safe to identify these two women, as some modern editors of the correspondence have done. There is no variation or interchange of name in Boniface's own letters; the two are kept distinct throughout. Eadburg was the daughter of a former king of the West Saxons and abbess of St Mary's Minster in the Isle of Thanet. She appears to have been distinguished for piety and sweetness of disposition, learning and artistic accomplishment. At Minster she trained the young Lioba, before the latter was transferred to Wimborne Abbey and subjected to the sterner discipline of Abbess Tetta, a sister of King Ine. This world of Anglo-Saxon learned "religious" was an aristocratic society, but one in which significantly Boniface felt completely at home. In 735 or 736 he wrote a brief note to Eadburg (*Ep.* 30), thanking her for her gift of books to "an exile in Germany" and asking for her prayers. He wrote again the same year (*Ep.* 35), thanking her for another gift of books and vestments, and desiring her to copy out for him "the Epistles of my master, St Peter the Apostle, in gold letters, to impress upon the eyes of the worldly men to whom I am preaching honour and reverence for Holy Writ, and that I myself may have ever before me the words of him who is my guide upon this road." The request for earnest and unceasing prayer is repeated in a letter (*Ep.* 65) written several years later (742–46), wherein the saint pours out his heart to her concerning the many crosses he has to bear. "On every side is grief and labour, fightings without and fears within. Worst of all, the treachery of false brethren exceeds the malice of unbelieving pagans."

The name of Bugga—a diminutive or pet-name common among Anglo-Saxon girls—first appears in an early letter (*Ep.* 14) coupled with that of her mother, Eangyth, abbess of a double-monastery of unknown location. Written in 719 or 720, it is an answer to one from Boniface sent from the Continent. It is a feeble effort, doleful in tone, though not without touches of pathos and true religious feeling. Eangyth is oppressed by the cares of office, the responsibility of the cure of souls—the monks of the abbey were apparently an unruly lot—and external troubles like poverty and the oppression of the secular power. She feels friendless and alone. Death has robbed her and her daughter of all their relatives and dear ones. They long to lay down their heavy burdens and to go on pilgrimage to Rome, but there are many who condemn the practice as involving a breach of their religious vows. Boniface apparently was among them, but the two nuns, ignorant of his opinions, ask for his help and guidance.

To judge from the letter written a year or so later in her own name (*Ep.* 15) and congratulating Boniface on the success of his mission preaching in Frisia, Bugga was a

woman of stronger and more attractive character than her
mother. It is a confident letter for a young girl, and filled
with the spirit of joy and loving friendship.

> "The power of my love grows warm within me, now
> that I recognise that it is through your prayers that I
> have reached this haven of peace and quiet. I have been
> unable to get hold of the Martyrology for which you
> asked me, but I will send it as soon as I can come by it.
> And you, beloved, comfort my lowliness by sending me
> some select passages from Holy Scripture, as you pro-
> mised in your sweet letter. I am sending you fifty shillings
> and an altar frontal, which are the best gifts I can
> manage. Small as they are, they are sent with great
> affection."

Evidently other letters had passed between them, and it
may be supposed that a regular correspondence ensued.
In one of these missing letters Bugga returned to the project
of a pilgrimage to Rome. In his reply (*Ep.* 27), to be dated
in, or a little before, 738, Boniface refuses to commit himself.
He leaves the decision to the lady. He recognised the purity
of her motives and evidently had a good opinion of her
common sense. "I would not presume on my own responsibility," he writes, "either to forbid your pilgrimage or rashly
to persuade you to it. I can only put the case as I see it." On
the one hand, it would be foolish to quit the monastic life
and put herself to the trouble and inconvenience of mixing
with strangers and worldly folk which a long journey to
Rome would entail: on the other hand, if she cannot find
peace of mind and freedom of the spirit in the cloister at
home, let her by all means seek them at the shrine of the
Blessed Apostles. She had better wait, however, until the
situation in Italy becomes more tranquil. In the meantime
let her begin making preparations for the journey, and then
wait calmly on the will of God. May God reward her for her
gifts! "You know that the long-standing friendship between

us shall never fail: farewell in Christ." The letter is a model of tact and prudence—but in his heart he probably knew she would go. From the evidence in King Æthelbert's letter, already cited (*Ep.* 105), it is certain that they met in Rome, probably on the archbishop's third visit in 738–9.

Many years later, when they had both grown old and their ways had long since parted, Boniface wrote again to the abbess (*Ep.* 94), an exquisite letter, breathing the pure spirit of Christian charity.

"In compassion for your tribulations and mindful of your kindnesses and of our ancient friendship I am sending you a brotherly letter of consolation and encouragement . . . Rejoice and be glad always, beloved sister, and thou shalt not be confounded. Scorn earthly trials with your whole soul, for all soldiers of Christ, of both sexes, have despised the storms and troubles and infirmities of this world, and counted them as naught, as St Paul bears witness . . . Rejoicing in the hope of a heavenly fatherland, hold fast, beloved, the shield of faith and patience against all adversities of mind and body. With the help of Christ, your bridegroom, perfect in your beautiful old age to the glory of God the building of that tower of the gospel, which you began in early youth, so that when He shall appear, you may be found worthy to meet Him in the company of the wise virgins, bearing your lamp with the oil burning."

This is the saint's last letter to her. The date of her death is uncertain, but she probably survived him for several years.

No account of Boniface's friendships with Anglo-Saxon nuns would be complete without some reference to Lioba, the most attractive and saintly character of them all, and the one who had the greatest affinity with the archbishop in mind and spirit. She was a woman of rare talents, combining an intellectual capacity unusual in her sex in that age, with practical gifts of leadership and organisation. Her learning was universally acknowledged, and her biographer,

F

Rudolf, a monk of Fulda, lays special stress on her mastery of the Scriptures and the Fathers and mentions also her interest in canon law and problems of chronology. In later life she was often consulted by the Frankish and German bishops on matters of faith and order, and her judgments in these questions invariably commanded respect. According to Rudolf her decision to leave her nunnery at Wimborne and to come to Germany was the sequel to a personal invitation sent her by Boniface. She was a tower of strength to him in the work of planting and organising the monastic life, and one of its most successful practical exponents as abbess of Tauberbischofsheim. It was the combination of strength and tenderness in her character that drew Boniface to her. More and more as he grew older he came to rely on her wisdom and experience, and on the eve of his last adventure in Frisia he sent for her, begged her never to give up her work in Germany, whatever the future might bring, and commended her to the care of Bishop Lull, his successor in the see of Mainz. Evidently he regarded her as his true spiritual heir, a link between himself and the German episcopate. After his martyrdom she occupied a privileged position among the leaders of the German Church. At the Frankish court too she was held in great respect and honour. She became the intimate friend and counsellor of Hildegard, the wife of Charlemagne, thereby establishing a personal link between the great archbishop and the great emperor. She lived to a ripe old age, and when she died in 780, she was buried with her beloved master at Fulda, but not in the same grave, as he himself had ordered. Lioba was a model nun, a great abbess and an expert in the life of contemplation. But her true greatness was essentially a greatness of character. She had a genius for bringing out the best in others, men and women, and perhaps the secret of her power is to be found, not in her moral grandeur, but in her humanity. "She was always gay", wrote Rudolf, her biographer, and this unusual tribute from a medieval author indicates the profound impression made on contemporaries by this trait in her disposition. There is a charming and naïve simplicity about the one letter we have of hers (*Ep.* 29), written to Boniface as a young nun at Wimborne in, or soon after, 732, but it contains a hint of the mature personality she would one day develop. The letter is worth quoting in full.

"To her most revered master, Boniface, endowed with the insignia of the highest rank, most dear in Christ and related to her by blood, Lioba, the lowest servant among those bearing the easy yoke of Christ, sends wishes for eternal salvation.

"I beg you of your kindness to remember the friendship which bound you long ago in the west country to my father, Dynne. It is now eight years since he was taken out of this world, so cease not, I beg you, to pray for his soul. Remember also my mother, Aebbe, who is your kinswoman, as you well know. She is still alive, but has long been suffering from a grievous infirmity. I am my parents' only daughter, and though unworthy, I would I might consider you as my brother, for there is no other man in my family, whom I feel I can trust as much as you. I venture to send you this little gift; not that it deserves your attention, but that it may remind you of my humble existence and bind us more closely to each other for all time in true affection, despite the great distance which now separates us. I entreat you, dear brother, to protect me with the shield of your prayers against the envenomed darts of the hidden enemy. Would you also be so kind as to correct the rustic style of this letter and send me a few gracious words of your own as a pattern? I do so long to hear from you. I composed the little verses appended here according to the rules of prosody, not in presumptuous vein, but in the endeavour to exercise any slender talent I may possess, and conscious of the need for your assistance. I learned the art from my mistress, Eadburg, who continues unremitting in her study of the Scriptures.

"Farewell; may you live long on earth, and more felicitously in heaven; making intercession for me."

The letter closes with an invocation of the Blessed Trinity in four lines of laboured Latin hexameters after the style of Aldhelm—a long way after. Certainly the *young* Lioba was more skilled in Latin prose than in verse.

Through the schools and libraries attached to his monastic foundations in Germany Boniface, as we have seen, was the chief agent in the transmission of Anglo-Saxon religious learning to the Continent. His literary works, especially the *Letters*, played their part in reinforcing and developing that tradition: not that he himself was distinguished as a stylist, although at his best, particularly in his later years, he wrote clear, fluent and forceful Latin, and in this he certainly excelled all his Anglo-Saxon contemporaries. It was rather because his letters gained a wider publicity than he himself had either intended or foreseen, so many and various were his correspondents. Assuredly Bugga and Lioba were not the only ones to take their master's treasured writings as models for their own literary exercises. His friends and disciples everywhere, and their pupils after them, turned them to similar profitable uses. In this way the *Letters* made a definite, if limited, contribution to that "revival of learning" in the Frankish Empire which was sedulously fostered by Charlemagne and came to fruition under his son, Lewis the Pious, in the middle years of the ninth century. For this reason, if for no other, Boniface may be acclaimed the forerunner of that other great English teacher and man of letters, who also spent the greater part of his life on the Continent, Alcuin of York. Moreover, the growth and spread of Anglo-Saxon religious culture overseas reacted favourably in course of time on the church in England, and this was not the least of Boniface's many services to Western Christendom.

The *Letters* are thus the chief source for the more intimate and personal side of Boniface's character, but they also reveal, between the lines as it were, the secret springs of his spiritual power, the quintessence of *Boniface the saint:* his habit of daily prayer and meditation on Holy Scripture; his constant and regular practice of the sacramental life; his faith in God, Whose will he accepted in unquestioning obedience; his complete confidence in God's purpose for him and in the reality of his vocation. These were the foundations on which he built his life, and his prodigious achievements as a Christian evangelist and ecclesiastical organiser and statesman rest ultimately, not on the superiority of his mental and practical gifts, not on his capacity for leadership nor on the energy, tenacity and initiative which he displayed in action, not even on his broad humanity and his genius for love and friendship, but on his sanctity. This is the golden thread which runs through the successive stages of his life and work—youth and missionary apprenticeship, apostolate and martyrdom—and binds them all in one.

The year 752 may be taken to mark the opening of the last phase in the long and arduous life of Boniface, for in that year he took the first step on the road to martyrdom. Having crowned Pippin king of the Franks and set in motion the reform of the Frankish Church he doubtless felt it was high time to quit the arena of ecclesiastical politics. But it was no easy or leisured retirement that he was contemplating, no retreat to his beloved Fulda or any other sanctuary of peace. Despite advancing years—he was now well over seventy—he was still very much a man of action and thought of his life in terms of his original commission from Pope Gregory II as an evangelist "at large". The years had brought no weakening of the missionary impulse. His project of preaching the gospel to the heathen Saxons had been stillborn and he showed no disposition to revive it; but Frisia, that bleak and barren land which had summoned him to his earliest adventures, began again to exert a magnetic pull upon his spirit. He resolved to return thither and endeavour to complete the conquest of its people for Christ by waging a missionary campaign in the eastern half of the country, which still remained largely pagan and independent of Frankish rule and influence. If he must die, let it be in the armour of a soldier of Christ. But before he could make plans for such an enterprise, he had to provide for the future of the Church in Germany. Above all there was the crucial question of the see of Mainz. He had long desired to be relieved of his diocesan duties. Already in 748 he had sought permission from Pope Zacharias to resign his see in favour of a younger man, but the pope in his reply (*Ep*. 80) had refused to countenance the proposal. The utmost concession he would make was to sanction the appointment of a bishop-coadjutor to take over the cure of souls and to relieve Boniface of the burden of routine administration, if a suitable man could be found among the *chorepiscopi*. Boniface had such a man in mind. He had long been training his fellow-countryman, Lull, as his destined successor in the see. But he knew that Lull's nomination would need confirmation from the Frankish king. So he petitioned Pippin through the influential Fulrad, abbot of St Denis (*Ep*. 93), to ratify the appointment and to accept Lull as his successor as head of the German mission. The king graciously acquiesced, and Lull assumed charge of the see, while Boniface returned grateful thanks (*Ep*. 107). The letter to Fulrad contained another request indicative of Boniface's anxiety for the safety and welfare of the host of disciples and fellow-countrymen, whom he had installed in bishoprics and abbacies in every corner of Germany, or who were actively engaged with him in the mission field. "It seems to me," he wrote, "considering my infirmities, that I must soon end this mortal life and cease the daily round of my activities. Wherefore I beseech His Royal Highness in the name of Christ, the Son of God, to inform me, while I yet live, what provision he is willing to make for my disciples hereafter. They are nearly all foreigners. Some are priests whom I have appointed in various places to take charge of churches and their flocks. Some are monks living in cloister, or children learning their letters. Others have grown old companioning with me and helping me in my work. I am anxious about them all, lest after my death they be dispersed and scattered abroad like sheep without a shepherd, unless they have Your Highness' support and patronage." Was Boniface moved to make this plea by an old man's natural desire to provide for every eventuality, or had he already a presentiment of his approaching death, such as Willibald specifically records in his account of the saint's last conversation with Lull on the eve of his departure for Frisia? We cannot tell. More significant is the evidence of his care and forethought for those who had shared his travails and his triumphs in Germany, and without whom, as he well knew, his work there could never have been accomplished.

The death of Pope Zacharias in March 752 and the accession of Stephen II made no change either in the situation in Germany or in Boniface's plans for the future. Nearly a year elapsed before he sent the new pope the customary letter of greeting and congratulation (*Ep.* 108). The delay was due, not to negligence or discourtesy, as the archbishop is careful to explain in the letter, but to his preoccupation with the task of rebuilding and repairing more than thirty churches pillaged and damaged or destroyed by the Saxons in a large-scale raid on Thuringia. But he is writing now to renew his pledge of love and obedience to the Roman Church. "For if I have achieved anything of value in this Roman mission in which I have been engaged now these six-and-thirty years, I desire to increase and fulfil it." One

more letter to the new pope (*Ep* 109), and Boniface's papal
correspondence closes. This was probably written early in
753, when preparations for the expedition to Frisia were well
advanced. It deals with a dispute between Boniface and the
bishop of Cologne concerning jurisdiction over the see of
Utrecht. Boniface rehearses for the pope's benefit the story of
Willibrord's mission to the Frisians and the foundation of
the bishopric. Later Carloman had entrusted the see to
Boniface and charged him with the duty of consecrating a
bishop. But now the see was again vacant, and the bishop of
Cologne had the effrontery to put forward a counter-claim
on the strength of an alleged privilege granted to one of his
predecessors by King Dagobert as far back as 639, though
none of the bishops of Cologne had made the slightest effort
to fulfil its conditions by preaching to the people or con-
verting them. This claim Boniface vigorously opposes, and
asks the pope to send him written confirmation of the
original grant made to Willibrord by Pope Sergius. As
Hauck pertinently remarks, "it was the last service Boniface
required from the pope". What response it evoked, if any,
is not recorded, but the dispute undoubtedly had the effect
of hastening Boniface's departure for Frisia. It was imperative for him to be on the spot in Utrecht as soon as possible,
and Utrecht was the obvious base for missionary operations
in the eastern province of the country. But it was equally
important to obtain the goodwill and support of the king of
the Franks, and the spring of 753 found the archbishop in
Neustria pleading his cause at the Frankish court. It was his
last interview with Pippin, and he was successful in his
quest. On 23rd May the king granted a privilege confirming
him as administrator of the see of Utrecht, thus effectually
disposing of the counter-claim of Cologne and settling the
issue. From Pippin's court Boniface made his way to
Utrecht, where he promptly installed one of his most trusted
Anglo-Saxon followers, the *chorepiscopus* Eoban, as bishop of
the diocese.

Parting from old friends and beloved disciples in Germany had brought sore anguish and anxious fears for his safety. Lull, in particular, whose lot it was to receive his master's detailed instructions concerning the building of new churches in Thuringia and the completion of the abbey church at Fulda, and to promise that after death the archbishop's body should be brought back there for burial, could scarcely control his emotion. And when the saint bade him pack in the chest of books which he was taking with him a linen sheet to serve him as a shroud, he broke down utterly. According to Willibald, in this atmosphere, charged with suppressed grief and unutterable misgivings, the saint himself was the calmest person among them and went on quietly and methodically with his preparations for the journey. In the late spring or early summer of 753 the expedition started. The archbishop and his small band of disciples, carefully chosen for the enterprise, took ship and sailed down the Rhine. At some point Boniface must have disembarked and gone on alone to Pippin's court in Neustria on the business already described. He probably rejoined the party at Utrecht about midsummer, but the chronology of this last Frisian campaign is uncertain and confused, mainly through Willibald's vagueness and the lack of precise evidence from other sources. From Utrecht the party made its way northwards through the marshlands towards the Zuider Zee and into the very heart of Frisian heathendom. In this region, Willibald tells us, much success attended the saint's preaching. With the assistance of Bishop Eoban, whom he had brought along with him from Utrecht, he employed the familiar technique of administering mass-baptism to all who were willing to renounce idolatry and worship Christ. Nor were his activities confined to preaching the gospel. His practical gift of organisation was manifested as powerfully as of old. Everywhere he set about repairing old ruined churches and building new ones, until the onset of winter forced him to desist and

retire, probably to Utrecht, perhaps even to Mainz. Next
year he was back, breaking new ground beyond the Zuider
Zee in the far north-eastern corner of the country, the
modern Dutch province of Friesland. He pitched his camp
at Dokkum on the banks of the River Borne, about ten
miles from the sea and about fifteen from the modern town
of Leeuwarden. Hither he summoned his newly baptised
converts to meet him on the feast of Pentecost to receive
from him the sacrament of confirmation. But at daybreak
on 5th June, as he and his companions were awaiting the
coming of the neophytes, the camp was attacked by a horde
of armed warriors belonging to a neighbouring heathen
tribe. Some of his servants hastily snatched up weapons and
tried to defend the archbishop and his clergy, but Boniface
rebuked them and bade them all prepare for martyrdom,
exhorting them with noble words of courage and consolation. It was a massacre in cold blood, and it is doubtful
whether there were any survivors. More than thirty of his
companions perished, including Eoban, and some other
Anglo-Saxons. A later tradition reckons the total number of
martyrs as fifty-two, including, no doubt, the servants.
Boniface himself received the fatal stroke while seeking to
shield his head with the book he had been reading in the
tent, "desiring to be defended in death by the book he had
loved to read in life", as the anonymous priest of Utrecht,
from whom this graphic detail is derived, quaintly puts it.
The sword pierced through both book and head, and the
old man fell lifeless to the ground. His death was thus no less
dramatic than his life, and he sealed his outstanding career
as an evangelist with a martyr's blood. After the massacre
the pagan barbarians, drunk with blood, if not with liquor,
quarrelled among themselves and turned against their
fellows the bloodstained weapons with which they had slain
the holy martyrs. Some of them ransacked the tents in a
vain search for food and drink and treasure, but found only
the saint's travelling library, whose precious manuscripts

they cast in their drunken fury to the four winds of heaven
or trampled underfoot in the marshy ground, whence a few
of them were later salvaged and brought back to Fulda.
Three of these can still be inspected in the State Library
there, including a damaged codex of the Gospels, written
in an Irish hand and traditionally identified with the book
the saint had used in an endeavour to ward off the mortal
blow.

The bodies of the saint and his martyred companions
were brought back across the water to Utrecht and thence,
despite the protest of the citizens who desired to keep them
there, by solemn stages up the Rhine to Mainz in the funeral
ship which Lull had sent for them. At Mainz crowds of
mourners thronged the cortège and here again the people
were loth to allow it to proceed on the final stage of its
journey to Fulda. Apparently many of the saint's friends
and disciples shared the opinion of the clergy and citizens
of Mainz that the saint's body ought to be buried in his
episcopal city. Lull himself was half inclined to agree, but
he dared not lightly disregard the dead man's express
wishes, which he had solemnly promised to respect. Pressed
by Sturm, the abbot, he finally consented to the interment
of the body at Fulda, and so Boniface came home in death
to the hallowed spot he had cherished above all others in
the evening of his life. He was buried in the new church of
the abbey, in the midst of the peoples of central Germany
to whom he had been the first to bring the gospel of Christ.
Soon his sepulchre became a shrine to which pilgrims re-
sorted to ask for his prayers and to praise and bless God for
his heroic and dedicated life.

This short account of St Boniface and his work opened
with a quotation from the tribute paid to his memory by
Cuthbert, archbishop of Canterbury, as head of the English
Church. It could not close more fittingly than with a second
quotation, from a private letter (*Ep.* 112) written to Lull by
another Englishman, Milret, bishop of Worcester, who had

but lately returned from a visit to Boniface in Germany when he learned of the martyrdom. Milret refers to the martyred apostle as "the glory and crown of all whom the Motherland has sent forth to the European continent." It might well serve as the saint's epitaph, for no man in his day did more to raise the structure of European unity on the foundation of the Christian religion than this Anglo-Saxon "Apostle of Germany". St Boniface was a great Christian and a great Englishman, but he was also a great European. Perhaps this is the most important lesson he can teach us in our own day.

NOTE ON THE YEAR OF THE DEATH OF ST BONIFACE

Extraordinary as it may seem, it is still impossible to establish with absolute certainty the actual year in which St Boniface suffered martyrdom. This is due, partly to the confused and vague chronology of contemporary writers— Willibald's *Life* is no exception—and partly to the discrepancy between the two traditions of the saint maintained at Mainz and Fulda respectively, which may be an echo of the quarrel between Bishop Lull and Abbot Sturm, which broke out some years after the death of Boniface. The tradition of Fulda placed the martyrdom in 754; that of Mainz, basing itself on Willibald's *Life*, in 755. The later date prevailed among historians until about fifty years ago, when Tangl, in a series of articles in German periodicals embodying his researches into the question, advanced substantial, but by no means conclusive, arguments in favour of 754. Pending the discovery of new material containing irrefutable evidence, the question is still very open. *The Church of England, following the Mainz tradition, has always accepted 755 as the official date.* There would seem at the present time to be no valid reason for departing from it. No doubt or dispute exists, however, about the day or the month on which the event occurred. This was 5*th June*.

RECOMMENDATIONS FOR FURTHER READING

Good short accounts of St Boniface may be found in M. Deanesly, *History of the Medieval Church;* C. Dawson, *The Making of Europe,* and notably in Sir Frank Stenton, *Anglo-Saxon England.* There is a good article by A. L. Poole in Ollard and Crosse' *Dictionary of English Church History.* Of the older accounts the best in English is that of J. P. Whitney in the *Cambridge Medieval History,* Vol. II, Chap. XVI (B), while the full-length survey of A. Hauck, *Kirchengeschichte Deutschlands,* Vol. I (unfortunately untranslated) remains unsurpassed. The standard work in English for the Anglo-Saxon missions to Europe as a whole is now W. Levison, *England and the Continent in the Eighth Century.* This may be usefully supplemented on the cultural side by S. J. Crawford, *Anglo-Saxon Influence on Western Christendom.* E. S. Duckett, *Anglo-Saxon Saints and Scholars* contains a charming biographical essay on St. Boniface. Of biographies proper G. Kurth, *Saint Boniface (680–755)* (in French) is to be preferred to Bishop E. G. Browne, *Boniface of Crediton and His Companions.* The collected correspondence of St Boniface has been translated into English by the American scholar, E. Emerton, *The Letters of St Boniface,* and C. H. Talbot, *The Anglo-Saxon Missionaries in Germany,* published only last year, contains a large selection from the saint's letters in English translation in addition to Willibald's *Life* in full and the *Lives* of Sturm and Lioba.

INDEX

Ælbwald, king of E. Anglia, 67

Æthelbald, king of Mercia, 66

Æthelbert II, king of Kent, 67, 71

Aidan, St, 7

Alcuin of York, 74

Aldebert, 55, 57

Aldhelm, abbot of Malmesbury, bishop of Sherborne, 10, 74

Alfred, King, 5

Allemannia, 37, 44

Amöneburg, 22, 35, 44

Aquitaine, 3, 52

Augustine, St, archbishop of Canterbury, 39, 64

Austrasia, 26, 51, 52, 55

Austrasian councils, 54

Bavaria, 37, 38, 46, 49

Bede, 6, 10

Bergit (or Bertha), 33

Bertwald, archbishop of Canterbury, 11

Binna, 23

Boniface, St, birth, 8

educated at Exeter, 9; ordained, 11; envoy to archbishop of Canterbury, 11; preaches in Frisia, 14, 15; returns to England, 15; sets out for Rome, 17; audience with Pope Gregory II, 17; receives Pope's mandate to preach in Germany, 18; renamed Boniface by Pope, 18; leaves for Thuringia, 18–19; joins Willibrord in Frisia, 19–22; preaches in Hesse, 22; summoned to Rome, 23; consecrated bishop for Germany, 24; visits Charles Martel, 25; receives Charles Martel's mandate, 26, 32; destroys Geismar oak, 27–8; letter from Gregory II, 29; missionary problems in Hesse and Thuringia, 30–

2; appeals for help from England, 32; progress in Hesse and Thuringia, 34–5; relations with Holy See, 36; made archbishop of Germany, 36; third visit to Rome, 37; receives Pope's mandate for Bavaria and Allemannia, 37, 39; in Bavaria, 39; relations with Odilo, duke of Bavaria, 40; organisation of Bavarian episcopate, 41; granted legatine authority in Germany, 42; summons council of Bavarian Church, 42; foundation of monasteries in Bavaria, 42; returns to Hesse and Thuringia, 43; creates new sees, 44; founds abbey of Fulda, 45–6; relations with Pope Zacharias, 49–51; given plenary powers over Frankish Church, 51–2; relations with Carloman and Pippin the Short, 52–6; reforms Frankish Church, 53–7; presides over Austrasian reforming councils, 54; measures against Aldebert and Clement, 55; holds general councils of Frankish Church, 55, 56; visits Frankish court, 58; crowns Pippin, king of the Franks, 59; dispute with bishop of Cologne, 78; last Frisian expedition, 79; martyred at Dokkum, 80; buried at Fulda, 81

the "Apostle of Germany", 2

a "son of Wessex", 4; exponent of Anglo-Saxon religious culture, 6; "spiritual son of Celtic monk-missionaries", 7; of noble birth, 8; demands for books in his letters, 64; legacy to Christendom, 82; literary legacy, 74; literary works, 10; personality and character, 60–4; patriotism, 63; sanctity, 75; views on pilgrimages, 63, 69–71; as an ecclesiastical organiser, 38, 53–9

correspondence of, 1, 10, 61–75; cor-